FROM THE RED ARMY TO SOE

From the
Red Army to SOE

Major L.H. Manderstam

with

Roy Heron

WILLIAM KIMBER · LONDON

First published in 1985 by
WILLIAM KIMBER & CO. LIMITED
100 Jermyn Street, London, SW1Y 6EE

© Estate of L.H. Manderstam, 1985
ISBN 0-7183-0588-4

Typeset by
Print Co-ordination, Macclesfield, Cheshire
and printed in Great Britain by
The Garden City Press Limited,
Letchworth, Hertfordshire, SG6 1JS

To my grandchildren,
God bless them,
for they shall inherit
the future.

Contents

List of Illustrations

Preface

Forty years after the Second World War a continuing stream of films, books and television programmes bears witness to the thirst for information about Britain's secret services and in particular the activities of Special Operations Executive, the sabotage, subversion and espionage organisation. SOE attracted to its ranks many men and women who displayed exceptional talent and strength of character, and none more so than Len Manderstam, a Russian-speaking consulting engineer whose particular brand of dynamism and independence of spirit made him ideal material for clandestine work, even though it led to numerous clashes with the authorities, as represented by the Foreign Office.

Most books about SOE have laid emphasis on the networks set up in occupied France, the main area of operations, but the organisation spread to every theatre of war. Little has been written about SOE's work in neutral countries, where Major Manderstam operated for much of his service and only the briefest of references have been made to West Africa and to Angola, where he formed an SOE section and took part in a series of extraordinary adventures. SOE's Russian section, of which he became head, also received scant attention from the historians and not until 1974 did his role as the officer who led the protests over the forcible repatriation of Soviet prisoners become public knowledge. Manderstam's protests and his forecast of what would happen to the prisoners eventually reached Winston Churchill, after being passed on by Lord Selborne, but intervention by the Foreign Secretary, Anthony Eden, ensured that the warnings were disregarded and the official policy was not changed.

Russia figures prominently in Len Manderstam's story because he was born there and in his formative years lived through the Revolution and its aftermath, an experience, coupled with a period spent in Africa, which dictated the course of his war service and his business career.

Always an individualist, he often created problems for his superiors by acting against orders. His refusal to be bound by time-worn conventions led to palpitations in Whitehall and murmurings of possible diplomatic repercussions, but his work as an SOE agent was known to the secret police of Portugal, Spain and the Portuguese colonies, even if they could not prove his involvement in specific acts of sabotage. Somewhere in the dusty archives of Lisbon and Madrid exist files about his various wartime missions. In Moscow, too, are kept details of his life, with special reference to the tragic episode in which the Allies delivered millions of people to the Soviet Union to face execution or internment. He was the first British officer to interrogate in depth Russians who had fought alongside Hitler's Army in the hope that they might defeat Bolshevism in their homeland, and the Soviet authorities have not forgotten his condemnation of the repatriation policy. What may come as a surprise to the KGB, however, are the disclosures in this book of his service as a Red Army colonel on the Eastern Front and of his imprisonment in the Lubianka. Major Manderstam told me there were at one time twelve files on him in the office of Sir Maurice Oldfield, head of MI6. But when, during the war, Manderstam began to give General Gubbins a detailed account of his Russian Army service and arrest by the Cheka, the SOE chief stopped him with the remark, 'For God's sake, Mandy, don't tell anybody.' He was certainly the only SOE agent to have served as a Red Army officer.

Major Manderstam had always refused to discuss his career. Then, as he neared eighty years of age, he felt the need to leave behind a record. Our mutual friend Captain A. R. (Dick) Cooper suggested a meeting and I wondered if the stories I had heard about Mandy might not be exaggerated – they seemed incredible. Such notions were dispelled when I met him, and I soon had no doubt he was one of the most remarkable secret agents of the war. We met regularly as he unfolded his life story: his part in the Russian Revolution, service in Trotsky's Army, his imprisonment for anti-Bolshevik activities; the years he spent in Africa and his recruitment to the Baker Street 'cloak and dagger gang'. Shortly before the war he invented a vegetable oil process which provided the capital to set himself up as a consultant. And he used his wealth and commercial contacts in the Allied cause, dipping deep into his own pockets when Whitehall refused to open its purse. After the war he developed his consultancy firm into a world-wide business with an annual turnover of millions of pounds.

He had two severe strokes while we were working on his memoirs. Although crippled and wheel-chair bound, he insisted on going to his office each morning and doing a full day's work, a truly prodigious feat for a man who was turned eighty. Sadly, Len Manderstam died before his life story could be published, but not before he approved the draft manuscript. His passing was mourned in many countries, particularly in the third world, where much of his business was conducted and where he was a friend and confidant of presidents and prime ministers. He also met a number of war leaders during his SOE service, including Field Marshal Smuts. Mandy disliked Smuts and yet acquired from him an endearing mannerism. Smuts usually ended conversations with a curt, 'Goodbye,' but if he liked and approved of someone he bade farewell with the words, 'God bless you.' They were the last words Mandy spoke to me.

After Mandy's death a number of former agents and other SOE personnel got in touch with me, raising questions I should like to have put to him. Did he, for instance, have a part in the arrest and execution of a German spy in 1943? The previously unrecorded incident demolished an assumption that agents were not in danger of their lives when they were sent to neutral countries. This particular spy was landed on the Angolan coast from a U-Boat but he was reported to the Portuguese authorities by SOE, strange as it may seem, and he was arrested before he could do damage. Early in the war, when they assumed the Germans would win, Portuguese officials in the colony were aggressive and obstructive towards the Britons living there. When the pendulum swung in the Allies' favour the officials changed their attitude to the extent of agreeing to hand over the German spy to a British representative. One of the SOE section in Luanda saw the German into the custody of an armed guard aboard a ship going to Cape Town, I was told by a reliable informant. And when he reached South Africa the agent was shot.

A debt of gratitude is owed to many people whose help has been invaluable in the course of preparing this book for publication. They include Joan Bright Astley, Captain A.R. (Dick) Cooper, Peter Dawson, Jean Ebstein-Langevín, Lady Gubbins, the Manderstam family, Frank Osmond Martin, Tony Mills, George Morgan, Peter Searle, Catriona Sopper, Count Nikolai Tolstoy, Sibyl Vincent, Laura Warner, and the staff of the Imperial War Museum.

ROY HERON

CHAPTER ONE

Early Days

In the spring of 1942 I returned to London from West Africa and for the first time became aware of a certainty, rather than a hope, of an Allied victory in the war against Nazi Germany. This feeling was not due entirely to the mild, burgeoning days of May and the tide of optimism which flows with the approach of an English summer. There was tangible evidence. The Battle of Britain had been won; London and the cathedral cities had survived unbowed the worst firestorms of the blitz, and the RAF was hitting back at the German heartlands with thousand-bomber raids on Cologne and the Ruhr. But perhaps most important had been Hitler's supreme blunder in attacking his former ally, the Soviet Union. Then, in December 1941, the Japanese, impelled by a similar outburst of lunacy, devastated the American naval base at Pearl Harbour. And so the two mightiest nations on earth were brought into the war on the same side.

Each day the newspapers and radio bulletins recorded the successes and reverses of the RAF, the Army and the Navy. There was a fourth armed service, however, whose deeds were never mentioned, except obliquely, and yet whose impact on the course of the war was vital. They wore no uniforms in battle and many of their number died heroically, unsung. For they were the men and women of Special Operations Executive, who fought behind enemy lines. Their exploits and the name of the organisation were kept secret until hostilities ceased. Even now there is much to be revealed about clandestine operations by SOE and the Resistance which, General Eisenhower maintained, shortened the war against Hitler by nine months.

Like most of my colleagues, I had become a secret agent almost by accident. My first mission was in the Portuguese West Africa colony (Angola) and soon after my return I walked up Baker Street

to the group of anonymous buildings which had been taken over by
the staff of SOE. My own office was in a red-brick block of
requisitioned flats at Montagu Mansions. The room allocated to me
was sparsely furnished with two desks, a couple of chairs and a
telephone, and I was sitting there, drinking my morning coffee,
when the 'phone rang. CD wanted to see me at 1400 hours I was
told and I knew better than to question the instruction because CD
was the symbol by which we knew Sir Charles Hambro, who had
recently taken over as head of SOE. Just what did he want me for?

Promptly at two o'clock I presented myself at Hambro's
headquarters, across the road at 64 Baker Street, where his secretary
informed me Sir Charles had been delayed elsewhere. For two hours
I sat twiddling my thumbs and speculating on the prolonged lunch,
brandy and cigars my chief was no doubt enjoying while his
secretary busied herself with the departmental routine. At last Sir
Charles arrived and invited me into his office. He obviously had no
idea who I was. There was an awkward silence as he stared at me
intently and then perused a note on his desk. He looked at me again
and, with a wry, apologetic smile, he said, 'I have been asked to
congratulate you, but I'm damned if I can remember what it's all
about.'

Barely suppressing my amusement I explained how, some time
before my recall to London, I had been responsible for the capture
of a Vichy French ship and its valuable cargo. Perhaps this was the
incident he had in mind? It was, and SOE's executive director said
it deserved a DSO.

The encounter was typical, and Hambro really did have a
shocking memory for SOE matters. A merchant banker and
chairman of the Great Western Railway, he was one of a number
of brilliant men from the City who joined Britain's secret service
during the Second World War. They helped to form as motley a
collection of people as could be imagined, drawn from many nations
and all walks of life. Most of us had been born overseas or had lived
for years in countries which had been overrun by the Germans and
it was this reservoir of experience that Winston Churchill sought to
use in carrying the battle deep into enemy-held territory. 'Set
Europe ablaze,' had been Churchill's first order to SOE, which was
later extended to include any occupied country or sphere of German,

(*Left*) Minna Manderstam (*née* Lippman), mother (*Right*) Herman Manderstam, father.

Suworow-Strasse, Riga, where L. H. Manderstam went to school.

(*Left*) Manderstam as a schoolboy at the time of the revolution. The officer-class epaulettes and insignia have been removed from his uniform. (*Right*) The French teacher whose wig was removed by Manderstam.

(*Left*) Kiselnikow, Soviet envoy in Cairo, during his schooldays, when he was one of Manderstam's 'gang'. (*Right*) A beach scene near Riga, where the Manderstams had a dacha.

Italian or Japanese influence.

I had been recruited to SOE because of my familiarity with Africa. Another reason the organisation was interested in me, it transpired, was my intimate knowledge of Russia, where I spent my first twenty-two years.

*

All my life I have had a reputation for being obstinate, although I prefer to call it a streak of determination. It was a reputation I gained while still within the womb, for I was a fortnight overdue in being born and my mother was in labour for three days before I arrived, weighing ten pounds, on 13 July 1903.

We lived in one of the large stone-built apartment blocks which stood in neo-Classical splendour outside Riga old town and my first memory is of an incident there when I was two years old. I had obtained from somewhere a police whistle and sat on a doorstep blowing the whistle until I was red in the face. Suddenly the regular clip-clopping of carriage horses on the tree-lined boulevards nearby was drowned by a thunder of hooves as a squadron of Cossacks galloped at full pelt. They swept into the quadrangle formed by the apartments and reined to a snorting halt when they saw the cause of the apparent distress call. One of the Cossacks dismounted. He grabbed the whistle and gave me a thorough spanking before sending me home. Such was the impact of my first brush with the representatives of authority that I have a clear recollection of the uniformed Cossacks, looking enormous and formidable on their horses. I also remember, perhaps because my mother made remarks about it, how I refused to shed a tear when the Cossack hit me.

Mother was an admirer of Leopold II, King of the Belgians, who was the driving force behind efforts to develop the Congo basin, and she named me after him. I hate the name. Leopold sounds so pretentious and I'm glad most people call me Len, although to my former service colleagues I have always been Mandy.

My father, Herman Manderstam, was born in South Africa of Dutch extraction. His parents were well-to-do and he became fairly wealthy in his own right by building up an international business specialising in hides. For some years he traded in South Africa, but he was later attracted by the opportunities available in Riga, which was a thriving Baltic city and the capital of the Russian region of Livonia.

There he met my mother, Minna (née Lippman), a Balt whose family came from the border area between Russia and Prussia and who was immensely proud of her origins. She was twenty-eight when they married, which was considered rather late for her generation, and she it was who ruled the roost as far as the family was concerned. A large monochrome portrait of my mother, which I took everywhere with me, gave a good impression of her strong willpower, emphasised by steadfast eyes and a determined chin.

Mother's forebears, the Balts, were an advanced and independent people long before the birth of Christ. In the late 18th century all Baltic lands came under Russian rule, a position which was never accepted by the subjugated people. Soon after the start of the present century their resentment erupted, particularly in Riga, which was the second largest port on the Baltic after St Petersburg. That was the situation when I was born, in a city where the people's agitation developed into actions against the Baltic Germans and against the landowners, a precursor of the Russian Revolution. There was considerable ill-feeling towards the Germans who had moved into Livonia. Of Riga's 337,000 population, 115,000 were Germans, outnumbering the Russians, the Letts and the Jews who also lived there.

Riga's history went back more than seven hundred years. I liked best the old town, which preserved the aspect of a medieval city, with dark, mysterious streets and ancient monasteries and churches, including St Peter's, whose steeple, a landmark for miles around, pointed four hundred feet into the sky. Ask anyone in the West what they know about Riga and they will probably recall very little – perhaps the two German invasions in this century and the heinous crimes committed during the Nazi Occupation. Some may refer to Riga's short-lived freedom, which came to an end with Hitler's Operation Barbarossa, and then the Soviet annexation of the Baltic States. But many will remember the limerick about a young lady of Riga who was swallowed by a smiling tiger, which I first came across when I was learning to read English:

There was a young lady of Riga;
Who rode with a smile on a tiger;
They returned from the ride
With the lady inside,
And the smile on the face of the tiger.

In my time, the only tigers we had were the two-legged variety who joined the Revolution, and I was one of them.

But through all the trials and tribulations I managed to keep my sense of humour, and being able to see the funny side of any situation, no matter how bad, kept me sane.

There is no need for me to dwell upon the details of the social and political upheavals in Russia and the Baltic States, but the background does need to be kept in mind to explain much of what happened in my life. Japan launched its war against Russia soon after I was born and by 1905 the mood of the Russian people was one of depression, with many workers joining strikes in St Petersburg, culminating in the 'Bloody Sunday' massacre when Tsarist troops opened fire on the crowds.

From an early age I was acutely aware of the class distinctions that dominated Russian society. At the top was Tsar Nicholas II, an absolute hereditary monarch, assisted by various councils of state. He ruled the second largest empire in the world, after the British Empire. Beneath him came the Duma, with provincial representatives, and so the structure continued down to the village elders. But basically there were four classes: the peasants, the farming landowners, the businessmen and the nobility. To be born into one or other of those classes was almost as inhibiting as the Indian caste system. There was another, less clearly defined group, to which my mother aspired – the intelligentsia. Of course, one was not born into that class. One had to earn entry.

Mother came from a highbrow family, who were all university graduates, and most of whom were closely involved in the academic life of Russia. (One of her cousins was the distinguished American writer and political commentator Walter Lippman.) At times she treated my father with a certain amount of disdain because she considered herself his intellectual superior, although he had spent one or two years at university. I recall her reading the philosophers, including Nietzsche, Schopenhauer and Kant, and her ambition for me was that I should not go into trade or business like my father but should become a doctor or a lawyer. She had similar ambitions for my brother, Benjamin, who was seven years younger than me, and for my older sister, Agatha, who was sent to Lomonossov Girls' College in Riga. I gave my mother no cause for optimism.

My parents impressed upon me that, to succeed in life, I must obtain a place at one of the leading schools, the Gymnasiums, which opened the routes to the universities, the professions and to the upper reaches of the Army and the Civil Service. There was considerable discrimination in Russian schools, mostly on the grounds of religion and race, and I was handicapped on both counts.

The religious background of my family was a terrible mixture, ranging from Greek Orthodox to Lutherans, whereas my parents and I did not profess any religion. When my parents enquired about entrance to the Gymnasium at Riga they found that non-Greek Orthodox Russians, which included us, were allocated only five places in every hundred. Furthermore, there was an entrance examination in which Greek Orthodox Russians were required to obtain three pass marks out of five, while all others needed to get all five marks before they were even considered for a place. My mother obtained the services of a private tutor, a member of the Gymnasium staff called Rudoff, who made me work for at least ten hours each day. He kept unusual hours, partly I suspect because my mother was paying him illegally. Sometimes he would arrive at our home after midnight and awaken me, forcing me to read Pushkin or Gogol. He answered my protests by telling me, 'You should be capable of reciting it in your sleep.'

Rudoff must have been a good tutor, because I secured one of those five non-Greek Orthodox Russian places and, at the age of nine, became a pupil at the Emperor Nicholai Gymnasium. The Gymnasium was organised on paramilitary lines and its pupils wore grey officer-style uniforms, with tunics, greatcoats, highly polished boots and military caps. We all felt enormously proud when we walked out in those uniforms. They made us feel we had arrived, that we were among the élite, and the illusion was completed by the policemen who saluted us when we passed them in the street.

Possibly because I belonged to a minority group at school, I had a compulsion to assert myself and to attract attention. I had not been at the Gymnasium very long when I played a cruel prank on a French teacher I disliked and who wore a wig. She had a habit of leaning against a window sill in the classroom, so I rigged up a contraption on the window frame, with strings and a hook, and at a strategic moment lowered the hook and whisked off her wig. The poor woman turned crimson and, grabbing back her hairpiece, dashed away in obvious distress.

I also formed a gang of six or seven boys, with whom I used to go into a large park close to the school in search of mischief. Our main targets were the women in decorative hats and the men wearing shiny toppers. We lay in wait among the shrubs and, as the couples strolled by, I darted out, knocked their hats off, and ran like mad. It was just schoolboy devilry, intended to provoke such remarks as, 'Manderstam is not afraid of anything.'

To my parents I was an enigma. My school reports were either very good or very bad; rarely were the reports indifferent. On one occasion when I took home poor marks my father said, woefully, 'You have been given everything. An excellent governess, a beautiful home, and you have the best food. Yet you don't make the slightest effort to get good marks . . .' I interrupted his lecture. 'All right,' I replied, 'then I'll make it cheap for you. I won't eat!' And for about seven days I went on hunger strike and refused all food.

With hindsight it is easy to understand my father's exasperation. And he did provide a large and pleasant home for the family. We had a living-in maid, electricity, hot running water and the luxury of a bathroom, at a time when most Russians, even in the cities, made do with the public baths once a week – if they were lucky.

CHAPTER TWO

I Join the Revolution

The war clouds in Europe seemed far away, until one day in 1914 I heard an engine and looked into the sky to see a Zeppelin with German military markings circling over Riga. Beneath the gas-filled envelope were suspended shiny aluminium goldolas and I could see faces at the portholes. There was widespread panic, although we children regarded the Germans' arrival with intense curiosity rather than fear, especially as it was the first airship we had seen. The Zeppelin dropped no bombs, probably because it was on a reconnaissance flight, and after several leisurely circuits it gained height and departed towards the German border. Next time, our elders told us, we might not be so lucky.

My mother, as usual, kept her nerve and it was she, not my father, who resolved that we should leave for St Petersburg, where we could stay with her stepbrother while she made up her mind about our ultimate destination. The German forces were then about two hundred miles from Riga; and St Petersburg was more than three hundred miles in the opposite direction. Mother was sure the German Army would make a beeline for St Petersburg, Russia's capital, but she wanted to discuss the situation with her stepbrother, my Uncle Maxim, whom she adored.

Uncle Maxim was a political animal, the editor of the two most influential Russian newspapers supporting the Cadet Party and he was a close associate of Paul Nikolayevich Milyukov, the founder and leader of the middle-of-the-road Cadets. (A history professor, Milyukov opposed the Bolsheviks and eventually went to France, where he became a leading newspaper publisher.)

We went by train to St Petersburg, rattling across the flat, slightly forbidding landscape, which was sprinkled with thin forests harbouring elk, wolves and bears. The journey was an adventure for Agatha, Benjamin and myself, travelling to the capital where we could see for the first time the huge boulveards and squares of which we had heard so much, and the Winter Palace, the centre of court life and of the city itself. When we arrived we found that Uncle Maxim had gone on vacation to his summer home in Finland, and we had the free run of his apartment until his return

My main concern was to see as much as I possibly could of St Petersburg and all my pocket money was spent on the horse-drawn cabs, the Isvoshik, as I went sight-seeing up and down the Nevsky Prospekt and along the banks of the River Neva and the marvellous canals. Ornately uniformed police controlled the busy traffic in the main streets and Cossacks and mounted police were on constant patrol.

Attempts were made, without success, to get me into one or other of the schools during the time we spent in St Petersburg. A cousin of ours, named Klein, who was fairly high up in the Civil Service, was asked to help. Unfortunately, the report I took with me from Riga was hardly a flattering one, and Cousin Klein told my parents he was too embarrassed to try to get me into a good school. The Nicholai Gymnasium report said I was a very difficult person, that I was interested only in history and geography and I was not disciplined, either emotionally or physically.

After eight or nine weeks we set off on the most exciting train journey of my young life, crossing the Steppes aboard the Moscow Express, hauled by a burgundy-coloured engine which had a tall funnel and a huge lamp on the front. The track went like an arrow for four hundred miles and my father explained the reason: when the Tsar was asked to choose a route for the new railway he slashed a straight line across the map, from St Petersburg to Moscow, and told the engineers to get on with it.

We stayed in Moscow only long enough to change trains and then we were off again, travelling further inland another two hundred and fifty miles to Nizhni Novgorod, Russia's gateway to the East, on the junction of the mighty Volga river and the Oka. Father knew the area well, as it was a major centre of trade and commerce. He always attended the Nizhni Novgorod trade fair, the largest in the world, which each summer, until it was stopped by the Bolsheviks, attracted to the city half a million people from many lands. We moved into a spacious apartment at Kanawino, on the other side of

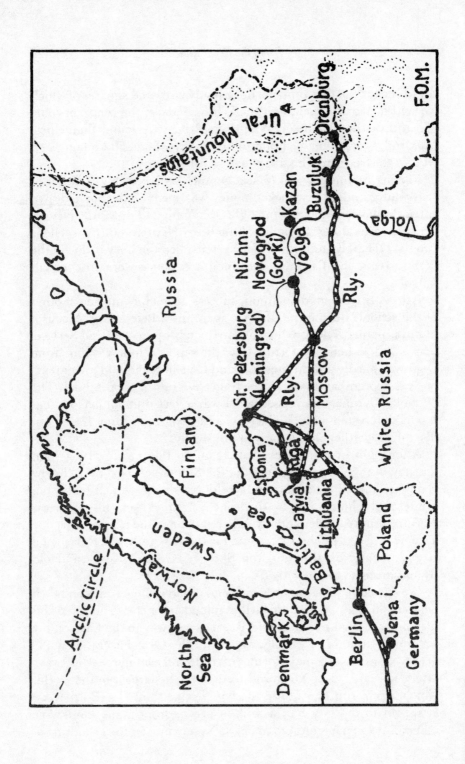

the Volga from Nizhni Novgorod town (which now, as Gorki, is closed to foreigners).

During the summer ferries carried passengers, goods and animals across the river. A bridge of boats linked the town to the tract of land on which were held the fairs that in two months provided Nizhni's livelihood for the rest of the year. In the winter the river ice was two or three feet thick and I loved to walk across the frozen river, which made a magnificent boulevard. Horse-drawn sledges could be hired, but it was much more fun to walk and to slide on the ice. Climbing up the steep streets and alleys to the upper town, more than two hundred feet above the Volga, we had a magnificent view of the beautiful countryside; the confluence of the Oka and the Vezloma, and the wide fields stretching away towards the Ural mountains.

Father bought a large tannery at Valdai, some miles away, and I was sent to the local Gymnasium at Kanawino. The school was much easier for a pupil to get into than the one in Riga. It also had a less rigid code of discipline. The two establishments were run on similar lines, however, and for me the military training was the most satisfying aspect of those otherwise tedious schooldays. Once again I found myself pushing to the front in any dispute; arguing and picking fights, although I must say I never quarrelled with anyone younger or smaller than myself. I found some familiar faces at the Gymnasium, for some of the teachers from Riga had been evacuated to Nizhni Novgorod shortly after the outbreak of war, including the French mistress whose life I had made a misery.

As we got older – and we aged tremendously in a couple of years – we turned away from childish pranks and concentrated on what we could do to help the war effort. Some of us tried to join the Army but we were rejected as too young for active service. Reports came in of political events in St Petersburg, where Uncle Maxim, through his Cadet Party membership, was particularly active. He was in favour of a democratic monarchy, and not a weak-kneed Tsar who held all the reins of power.

The war against Germany was going badly for Russia. Indecisive leadership, profiteering and a chronic lack of food, weapons and materials added fuel to the flames of revolution. Discontent among the civilian population was echoed and magnified at the Front, where tens of thousands of starving, ill-equipped soldiers were being massacred by well-fed, well-clothed, efficient and superbly armed German regiments. It was ideal tinder on which Lenin and Trotsky could throw sparks. Their arguments had an undeniable ring of sincerity, truth and fairness which formed a heady mixture. Political parties were fragmented and new factions seemed to appear every day, each one arguing its case in a most aggressive way and we maturing schoolboys were prime targets for the propaganda.

Students as a group, through the very nature of their environment and developing sense of social justice, have always been in favour of radical changes in society, and we were no different. When the Revolution finally broke in 1917 we were ready for it and at the forefront of the demonstrations, cheering the speakers, urging on the crowds, distributing pamphlets and helping in a hundred and one ways to fan the blaze.

Early in the year we had heard and read about the strikes and mass gatherings signalling the overthrow of the Tsarist regime in St Petersburg, which had by then changed its name to the less Germanic Petrograd. We cheered to the echo each step along the way to a workers' paradise. The abdication of the Tsar in favour of his brother, Michael, was followed almost immediately by Michael's abdication; and then we heard that the Provisional Government had been established.

We decided to take a hand by forming a school militia, of which I was appointed the leader. Red armbands were issued to each of our members. We had no weapons at first, so we took some from the Army arsenal – it was as simple as that. All we did was to go to the barracks in our pseudo officers' uniforms and tell the soldiers we wanted weapons for our militia, and they allowed us to take as many rifles and as much ammunition from the arsenal as we wished. Perhaps it was the Prussian blood in my veins, inherited from my mother's side of the family, that made me, as a boy, dream of leading a charge and dying a hero's death on the battlefield, or in front of a firing squad, as the 1812 Overture blasted away in the background.

I set as our school militia's first assignment an attack on the prison at Nizhni Novgorod and the release of all political prisoners held there. Off we marched across the frozen river towards the city, which dominated the far shore. As we climbed the hill into the upper city a wonderful panorama was spread beneath us, with the domes of the cathedrals gleaming in the sunshine. Far below were the frozen rivers Volga and Oka, with the black, animated specks of people stark against the ice. We saw the massive walls of the Kremlin, towering between sixty-five and ninety-five feet, and I was glad we did not have to storm them.

Along the way we sang and shouted slogans, our breath spurting like smoke from young dragons in the cold air. People ran from their homes and workplaces to join us, so that by the time we reached the prison we were at the head of a noisy mob, several thousand strong.

To our surprise and disappointment (as we had been looking forward to a scrap), the gaolers opened the gates without demur and let the prisoners out into the yelling crowd, where they were back-slapped and bear-hugged nearly to death. We convinced each other it was our red armbands, rifles and obvious revolutionary fervour that had secured the release of the prisoners. But it was more probable the guards, and the soldiers in the local barracks, were supporters of the Revolution and, in any case, were not looking for trouble when no one knew which party would gain control of Russia.

As the year progressed Lenin arrived from Switzerland; then Trotsky from America, giving his support to Lenin. Kerensky, as War Minister, ordered the ill-fated offensive against the Germans and, even though it failed disastrously, he still became head of the new Government in July 1917.

In our school life we developed into proper young Bolsheviks, organising everything through a soviet. I was already chief of the militia and found myself appointed chairman of the soviet. Not that I canvassed for either of these posts; it was taken for granted I would be in control and when asked, I accepted the jobs, which might sound arrogant but merely reflected my youthful confidence.

The whole atmosphere of the Gymnasium changed. Each class formed its own committee, with representatives on the school soviet, and delegates from the pupils attended meetings of the teachers. This changed situation might not have been welcomed by the staff, but they went along with it, even to the extent of altering their uniforms, as we did ours, to make them appear to be more plebian outfits. Epaulettes, braid and any insignia that set us apart from the workers were removed. Our workload was cut dramatically and most of the examinations were abolished. Certificates were handed to us without any test of our academic ability and the whole discipline of the school collapsed. Without exception, the teachers gave the appearance that they did not mind what was happening, yet they could not all have been Bolsheviks. More likely they, as with the soldiers and the gaolers, were terrified of what might happen in Mother Russia during the next few months.

Throughout all this, Uncle Maxim and the Cadet Party were busy. They were included in the Second Coalition Government, under Kerensky. A month or so later I heard the sad news that the Germans had taken Riga, my hometown, and were pressing on towards Petrograd. There were so many issues, so many sides, so many conflicts and it was difficult at times to know who was the real enemy. There was even talk that Lenin was helping the Germans and Trotsky's role was not clear, although in August Trotsky's group had thrown in their lot with the Bolsheviks. By November, of course, the Bolsheviks had taken over and Kerensky had gone.

I had been given my leaving certificate from the Nizhni Gymnasium without passing any examination or doing any work for it and when, under the rules, I was too young to qualify. This was my passport to university but first I resolved to play a more significant part in the Revolution. Another crack at joining the Army seemed a good way to achieve my objective.

CHAPTER THREE

A Self-Made Colonel

Although I was a large youth, six foot two inches tall and with the self-confidence to go with my height, I believed I could not bluff my way into the Army without producing a birth certificate. I was still too young, officially, for active service but I overcame that hurdle by the simple expedient of changing the date, adding two years to my age. I might have saved myself the trouble, because the new regime was not very bothered about such niceties and the authorities did not look too closely at my application. In any case, few people in the Army could read and write. By the time I joined up it was well into 1918 and the uniform I wore was that of the Red Army, under Trotsky.

It was a nasty business. The closing stages of the war against Germany mixed up with the civil war in which Russians were killing one another, Red against White, the Whites including the Cossacks from whose ranks had been drawn those dashing, if often callous, defenders of the Tsar.

I had a cousin, Jacob, who was called up as a medical officer, stationed in the Orenburg region of Eastern Russia and I had sought his assistance in getting a posting with the Army. He told me to go to Busuluk, a Cossack settlement in his sector, where he was sure I could enlist in the First Army of the Eastern Front, named after Comrade Trotsky.

There was a snag: Busuluk was several hundred miles from Nizhni Novgorod and I would have to make my own way there, at my expense. This meant an arduous journey eastwards by boat along the Volga to Kazan, former home of the Tartar Khans, and then southerly to Samara and the final leg by train towards the foothills of the Ural Mountains. My family was in no position to help me, even if they had wanted to support such a foolhardy venture, and I set off with virtually empty pockets. In fact money would have been of little use. It was almost valueless in a country where, in most areas, food could not be purchased at any price. The only sure way to obtain food or other goods was to barter for them, or to steal.

It took the steamer nearly a week to reach Kazan, during which time I and the other passengers became hungrier and hungrier, for there was no food on board. When we docked at Kazan for a stay of a couple of days I took the opportunity to hunt for something to eat. Nothing was available to buy or barter and so I stole from a field about twelve pounds of potatoes, scraping them from the ground with my hands. Such was my hunger I felt no guilt about taking someone else's food. I hurried off with my precious haul and lighted a fire in woods nearby, intending to boil some of the potatoes in a can, but in my state of near starvation I could not wait and bolted down several of them raw. I concealed the remaining potatoes in my clothes and they kept me going during the rest of my journey to Samara and on to Buzuluk. Those raw potatoes were all I had to eat for two weeks. Without them I would have been in a sorry condition indeed.

The Army units in the Busuluk area were completely disorganised and it was an easy matter for me to attach myself to a Construction Unit, which had the task of setting up field hospitals and sanitary units and Finnish-style sauna baths, the last to give soldiers an opportunity to relax and free themselves of lice and mud. Squads of axemen provided the logs that were our basic building materials, and we used a 'mortar' of mud, which was pushed into the gaps and crevices and which also helped to bind the straw we used on the roofs. Inside the bath huts were large, shallow metal containers of water. We heated stones on a fire outside and shovelled the hot stones into the water to create steam. Soldiers sat naked and sweating on raised wooden planks, occasionally splashing some of the water on to themselves and switching their bodies with birch branches.

Most of the soldiers were illiterate men, willing to be led, and it did not take me long to become chief of the construction unit. For good measure I gave myself the rank of colonel, making me, at fifteen years of age, almost certainly the youngest full colonel in the Red Army! It was unofficial and without authority from Moscow, but then few of my fellow officers had been through any test or form of assessment.

In the Tsar's Army the officers had worn gold epaulettes, which became hated symbols during the Revolution and they were forced to tear off their epaulettes to preserve their lives. The Red Army when it was constituted would have nothing to do with such insignia of power and privilege. Instead Red Officers had little squares on the cuffs of their uniform jackets, indicating their rank.

I stitched four squares on to each of my sleeves and no one questioned my overnight jump to the rank of colonel. The peasant soldiers were glad to have someone, even a young upstart, in charge and the officers were only too pleased to have another person accepting responsibility and taking some weight off their shoulders.

I was in the Red Army for about eighteen months, during which time my Construction Unit built dozens of field hospitals, sanitary units and bath houses. At first I was constantly shocked by the sight of the wounded, some with terrible injuries and others dying from gangrene after sustaining comparatively minor wounds that today would have been cleared up quickly by doses of antibiotics. I do not believe I ever became completely inured to the sight of men dying in agony, but it was necessary to develop a certain detachment or one would have gone crazy.

We worked constantly just behind the combatants. I did not take part in any of the fighting, although I witnessed a number of full scale battles and many lesser skirmishes. And I walked among the wounded and dead when the fighting abated. In winter the dead lay for days where they had fallen, literally frozen into grotesque postures. Any warm clothing was stripped from the bodies and put to better use, long overcoats and boots being particularly sought after. We had five or six months of frost but the snow set hard and dry, so that felt boots were the perfect footwear and warmer, if less smart, than polished leather. During the winter the region must have been one of the coldest places in Russia and yet it was hot in summer, the seasonal extremes of temperature being greater than in Moscow.

Month after month we toiled away, cutting down trees, transporting the timber on horse-drawn wagons and sledges and erecting the buildings, sometimes under fire. There were no established front lines, with settled battle patterns and well-worn trenches as there were in France and Belgium, and we were often in danger from Cossack raiding parties. No Cossack patients were to be seen in our hospitals, however, for the simple reason that the Red Army did not believe in taking prisoners; they shot them, or ran them through with swords. The same applied on the Cossack side, where thousands of captured Red soldiers were summarily executed.

Yet amid the carnage and obscenity of civil war I fell in love for the first time. She was a baroness, a beautiful girl known to us as Mary, who worked as a nurse in one of the field hospitals built by my unit. When I close my eyes I can still see her long blonde hair and deep blue eyes and a smile that would melt any man's heart. A Balt of Prussian descent, Baroness Margaretta Adalheim was careful not to disclose to the Bolsheviks that she had upper-class connections. My feelings for her were reciprocated and we walked for hours under the stars, holding hands and trying to ignore the debris of warfare.

She told me how she had been caught up in the Revolution while staying in Petrograd, where to save her life she had become a nurse for the Bolsheviks, picking up her medical knowledge as she went along, for she had no training. I was head over heels and I sought flowers for her eighteenth birthday, but there were no florists' shops in Busuluk. I knew she would be just as happy with flowers of the field, and that evening, after dusk, I crept out of my quarters, carrying a wicker basket borrowed from the hospital laundry room, and I filled the basket to the brim with lilies-of-the-valley that grew in profusion on the shady slopes. It was a fine night and the white, nodding flowers stood out clearly on the hillsides. I shudder to think how my comrades would have reacted if they had seen me, but the response I received from my little baroness made the risk worthwhile.

As an officer I had few perquisites and the only privilege of value enjoyed by any of us in the Army was to be able to send forty pounds of flour to our families each month.

One of my tasks as a Red officer was to commandeer the homes of Cossacks for use as Army billets. There were no such things as officers' messes and all ranks mixed in together as far as possible, but some were more equal than others, even in this emerging Bolshevik empire. Officers obtained a little privacy by taking over

Class of 1917 at Nizhni Novgorod Gymnasium. The city, as Gorki, is now closed to foreigners. L. H. Manderstam is second from right, back row.

Family group, at Riga, showing L. H. Manderstam (standing, left). Standing alongside him are a friend, L. H. Manderstam's brother, and their sister. Sitting are, from the left, an uncle and aunt, Mrs Manderstam and Mr Manderstam, senior.

(*Left*) Riga street scene. (*Right*) Cossack Guard, St Petersburg.

Nevsky Prospekt, the main street of St Petersburg (Leningrad).

Cossack shacks for their personal use. When I came to requisition a property for myself, I did not have the stomach for the job, even though in other matters I was absolutely ruthless. As an officer, I must not let the hard-bitten soldiers of the Revolution see how soft I could be, so I entered a wooden-built Cossack *chata*, but arranged to sleep outside on the verandah, leaving the family to the comfort of their home. It was no hardship, as I was young and strong and it happened when the nights were warm. The family had no beds as we know them in the West. They occupied one large room, in the centre of which was a brick stove and around the stove were arranged wooden benches, on which they slept.

The Cossacks were astonished when I did not turn them out. They welcomed me to their meals, at which the half dozen members of the family sat on the benches, round a large dish full of food and each person had a spoon. The first to take a spoonful was the head of the family, followed by the guest and then they took it in turns until the dish was empty. The biggest compliment they paid to me was to say, 'You are a Red devil, but at least you seem to be human.' Our Cossack opponents were spread across a number of regions, including the Don Cossacks and Orenburg Cossacks, whom we faced at Busuluk. They could be identified by the different coloured stripes on their trousers. Both sides were merciless in their approach to the internecine conflict.

There was a particularly disgusting episode that made me physically sick. A detachment of Cossacks raided a Red Army hospital near Busuluk during the night and raped and killed all the nurses. Not content with that, they hacked to pieces the male medical staff and also the patients in their beds. Then they dragged the still warm bodies of the nurses to the bank of a shallow river that ran by the hospital and slashed off their heads with sabres. The Cossacks placed the torsos by the edge of the river, so the nurses' blood drained into the water and was carried towards our quarters. The hospital was far enough away for us not to hear the noise of the slaughter and the first we knew of it was when we awoke next morning and saw the river was stained red.

Trotsky, as the Red Army chief, ordered instant and devastating retaliation. I had seen him only once, addressing a gathering of soldiers, but I knew him to be a man of action, a brilliant speaker and a confirmed Marxist from an early age. Trotsky personally launched an investigation. He demanded to know the name of the Cossack murderers' home village. A name was given to him – none of us was sure the Cossack raiders all came from that one place – and Trotsky ordered it to be wiped off the map.

I was told by the senior officer to lead an artillery force in an attack on the village. The military fervour of my schooldays had long since evaporated, but it was more than my life was worth to question such an order, authorised by Trotsky himself.

We marched overnight and arrived at our destination as dawn was breaking. Our field guns were ranged on high ground and foot soldiers encircled the rustic settlement. The only signs of life in the slumbering village were wisps of smoke from the embers of wood fires and the occasional stirring of horses. All was changed by the first volley of shells. As in a bad dream, I heard myself give the command to fire at will. I felt numb and completely drained as I watched the onslaught, which continued until every one of the closely-packed huts was razed. Cossacks who attempted to flee from their homes were mown down by rifle fire and as the sounds of the last volley died away the screams and shouts of wounded and terrified people were carried to us on the wind. Then the soldiers advanced through the acrid smoke to finish off with rifles those Cossacks who were still alive.

I estimate between six hundred and seven hundred men, women and children died on that terrible day. Why my fellow officers chose a militarily inexperienced teenager from the Construction Unit to be in charge of the punitive expedition was never explained. I did not know one end of a field gun from the other and almost the only commands I gave were the orders to fire and to cease fire.

That was the only offensive action in which I took part on behalf of the Red Army. I had stared into the true face of war and I was nauseated with what I saw.

It was no more difficult to arrange my release from the Army than it had been to get in, but such matters took time. The device I used was to change the wording of an official telegram which arrived from Moscow, informing us that Finland and Russia had come to peace terms and ordering the demobilisation of Finns serving in the Red

Army. As it happened, all telegrams came to me for processing and I altered the word Finland to Livland, the old name for the Baltic state of Livonia, of which my birthplace, Riga, was a part. The hardest decision I had made in my life up to then was to leave my baroness. We bade a long, and in her case tearful, farewell at Busuluk and I do not know what became of her.

While I waited for my discharge I went to Orenburg, a large town and capital of the province with the same name, where I noticed a considerable amount of vandalism and looting. Sporadic outbursts of shooting echoed around the town. With some of my comrades I rested in the former home of a rich merchant, where the lavishly furnished rooms were fitted with large, ornately framed mirrors and crystal chandeliers. Bolshevik soldiers to whom life behind the great doors of such houses had been an awsome mystery now found tremendous fun in throwing ornaments or bricks – anything that lay to hand – at the mirrors and chandeliers.

All the floors were littered with broken glass and bits of what had once been lovely and valuable porcelain figures and china crockery. We knew not what had happened to the merchant. He had either fled to safety or he was one of the countless thousands who were slain.

Among the most enduring memories of my service in the Red Army are the atrocities committed by both sides and of a speech by Trotsky. I have a vivid recollection of that most unmilitary-looking man in drab uniform, addressing his First Army of the Eastern Front in fluent, educated Russian. The only insignia I remember on his uniform was the red star pinned to his cap. Trotsky had a strong personality and there was no mistaking the fire in his belly as he stood on a rostrum in the open air to give a rallying speech to about eight thousand troops. I was a single pace away from him as he spoke on the theme of 'We must defend the Motherland at all costs. We are surrounded by enemies . . .' The performance was impressive and the cheers were spontaneous and deserved. As a speaker, Trotsky outshone Lenin and, compared with both of them, Kerensky was an also ran. I once saw Kerensky give a speech in Moscow and found him to be a weak character, completely unconvincing in his arguments.

CHAPTER FOUR

Against the Bolsheviks

My cousin, the Red Army doctor, accompanied me on the week-long train journey back to Nizhni Novgorod. By coincidence he had been given leave and it was doubly fortunate because he obtained for us some privacy by putting an official notice on our section of the crowded train, saying we had infectious diseases. People were dying like flies of typhoid, so we were left alone. We slept as much as possible, but one could hardly describe the conditions as comfortable. There were no passenger trains. This one was made up of covered trucks, each scheduled to carry forty men or eight horses and with 'windows' that were no more than square holes inset with iron bars and covered by hessian sheets. We slumped on the floor of one of these trucks, which we had to ourselves, tossing and turning with the discomfort of the hard, bucking planks and the irritation of lice and fleas and the malodorous stench of it all.

Both my parents were pleased to see me, especially as I had managed to obtain a large basket of fresh eggs to supplement their diet. Lack of food was their greatest problem, although my father was also considerably dispirited by the loss of his business. He was a disciplinarian and his unbending approach to his workforce ensured they had little sympathy for him when the Revolution came. If anyone asked for a rise, his stock reply was, 'I am not going to give you any more money because you will only spend it all on vodka'. In truth there was a considerable amount of drunkenness among the workers.

Father's idea of a treat, instead of increasing the men's wages, was to arrange for monks from a nearby monastery to visit the tannery, carrying with them an ancient icon. He thought it would give the workers a spiritual uplift and he failed to see, until too late, that the Church no longer held sway, for his employees were under the spell of the powerful message preached by the Bolsheviks.

The foreman at the Valdai tannery was an ingratiating Uriah Heep of a man called Alexander, who prefaced any remarks to, or about, his employer with the words, 'My boss.' I suspected Alexander had a sinister side and wasn't at all surprised to hear he picked up extra money by killing the local dogs, skinning them and selling their hides to the tannery. One night Alexander hammered on the door of my father's dacha, emboldened by drink, and shouted, 'We are short of hides – I'm going to skin you!' Gone was the submissive employee we knew so well. Father took one look at the long knife Alexander brandished and decided there was no future for any of us in Valdai. The factory was abandoned to the Bolsheviks, who requisitioned all our property, including the dacha. Father went back to Nizhni Novgorod, where my mother had stayed with my brother and sister.

I had some pleasant memories of summer days spent at Valdai. It was there that my father gave me a horse, which I trained with bribery. The countryside in those parts was very beautiful and I became a proficient horseman, riding miles in exploring the area. Everyone admired the way the horse followed me around like a trained dog. That was not due to my magnetic personality but to the sugar I always carried in my pockets.

Close to the factory was a big lake, the water cool, clear and inviting. But I could never swim because I had an inborn fear of water. This went back to when I was three or four years old nd my father decided to teach me to swim. We had a seaside dacha on the Baltic coast near Riga, and while spending a holiday there my father carried me into the sea beyond my depth and just dropped me in. I nearly drowned, and ever since have had a terror of water.

In the middle of Valdai Lake was a wooded island on which stood, at some distance apart, a monastery and a convent. For me it was always a place of mystery and I imagined the Brothers and Sisters going about their devotions, separate and celibate and isolated from the world. According to the local people, when the Revolution came the workers raided the two religious communities and discovered the buildings were connected by a tunnel. It was clear the tunnel was much used by the monks and nuns and there was evidence of orgies having taken place and the burial of babies, or so I was told. The monks and nuns were all either shot or imprisoned.

I got on well with the workers at the Valdai factory before the Revolution. They could see I was fond of animals, particularly my horse, which gave us a subject of mutual interest to talk about. Also they respected anyone who was educated. If there were anything they needed, or if they had a grievance, the men often used me as an intermediary, saying, 'Why don't you talk to your father about it?' But I never worked in the factory, much to my father's disappointment. (A similar situation faced my own son, Andrew, many years later, when I attempted to persuade him to join my organisation. He went to Westminster School and I put him in the science stream, to prepare him to join me in my work. He was totally unsuited for it, however, and chose to steer an independent course. He told me, 'I don't want to be the boss's son. I'm not going to do what you are doing. Whatever I build up, it will be my own.' I admired him for his determination to carve his own career in journalism and broadcasting.)

*

When I returned to Nizhni Novgorod after my Army service I found the mood of the city had completely changed. Long queues of gaunt people snaked along the pavements, waiting to collect the starvation rations of a small piece of bread and possibly some yoghurt and potatoes. My father went to Moscow to see if he could scrape together a living, and I joined him. If anything, the situation in Moscow was worse. The same air of depression pervaded the streets and all the euphoria of the Revolution had evaporated like a morning mist. We joined the queues for unpalatable hunks of black bread and we also obtained some potatoes. Only a starving person can know how delicious a baked or boiled potato can taste. The supplies were very erratic, however, despite a flourishing black market. Looking at my father's drawn face I was sorry for him, a feeling that was new to me. Sometimes when he returned to the room we shared, having not eaten all day, I pretended I had already had my fill and gave my potatoes to him.

Our troubles were as nothing compared with the fate which befell Uncle Maxim Ganfmann. He and some of his Cadet Party colleagues were arrested in Petrograd and given a rough time by the Bolsheviks. He was released from prison and went to Riga, where conditions were tolerable, as the Baltic States had asserted their independence from Bolshevik Russia. Paradoxically, he died through over-eating. I suppose, after his terrible ordeal in prison, the urge to cram his stomach was irresistible, and it affected his heart.

In Moscow, I thrashed around for something to do. I enlisted at the Mining Institute, whose students still wore pre-Revolution uniforms and which appeared to offer a chance of adventure. I had a vision of myself going to the Urals and the ends of the earth, searching for gold and other precious metals. After six months of monotonous work, studying textbooks until my head ached, I seemed no nearer my goal and the vision faded. I took a train back to Nizhni Novgorod to see my mother. Her strong words and common-sense failed to assuage my restless spirit and again I felt the need to take some part in political events. Moscow was the centre of things, so I returned to the capital.

By this time I had become completely anti-Communist. Each day we opened the Bolshevik newspapers to read proud boasts that three thousand people had been shot in one area, another two thousand elsewhere. Their crime: they belonged to the *bourgeoisie*. Armed Bolsheviks roamed the streets, rounding up people and examining their hands. If their hands were not calloused, they were accused of being *bourgeois* and many were put against walls and shot. I had already had a lucky escape through my friendship with a young rebel called Kabok. In deadly seriousness we planned a coup, which we intended would begin with a raid on the Communist headquarters at Nizhni Novgorod, where we would shoot all the officials. Fortunately for me, the scheme never materialised because Kabok contracted typhoid and died before we took the first steps.

Soon after my return to Moscow I was thrown into prison, accused of being a counter-revolutionary, and I came within a whisker of the firing squad. There was a huge groundswell of opposition to the Bolsheviks, especially among the intelligentsia, who saw that the Revolution had taken a wrong turn and was not leading to the promised land. Various dissident groups were active in Moscow and I began to take an interest in them.

A group I joined was officially a cultural organisation whose declared aim was to help the Jews in their fight to create a State of Israel. This was a safe enough 'front' because a high proportion of the ruling class – including Trotsky, Zinoviev and Rodzianko – were Jews and anti-Semitism was unknown in Moscow. Our organisation had a meeting on 14 April 1920, which we claimed was to examine the Jewish question, but which was really to discuss the injustices of the new Soviet regime. More than a hundred people attended the meeting but, unknown to us, our group had been infiltrated by secret police from the dreaded Cheka, the All Russia Extraordinary Commission. The Cheka had been set up as soon as the Bolsheviks seized power. Its very name struck terror into people's hearts and it spawned a series of equally feared organisations, including the OGPU and the NKVD.

No sooner had our discussion started than the doors were thrown open and we were surrounded by troops and armed Cheka agents. They bundled us into lorries, with many a push from rifle butts, and we were driven to the Lubianka. This was the road which we knew had been travelled by thousands of Russians who were never seen again.

We were kept in a yard outside the Lubianka, chilled to the bone, for a couple of hours and then placed in a cellar, a hundred and seventeen of us. There we exchanged the cold of the night for the sweaty warmth created by our own bodies. Conditions were extremely cramped, we were unable to lie down at full stretch and we slept, or rather dozed uneasily, in batches, crouched on the floor. When I plucked up courage and complained, the guard on duty gave me a sardonic smile and said, 'Don't worry. You will not live very long.' Every time the cellar door rattled we swivelled round, expecting at any moment to be herded out to face a firing squad. In the morning, guards came with unwholesome bread and weak tea, which became our sign of hope; if they were feeding us they would not be killing us that day. In the evening we were given a stinking liquid described as 'soup', and some bread. And so it went on, day after day. Twice a day we were allowed to go to the toilet, a most unhygienic place and for those that could not wait buckets were placed against a wall of the cellar. We had been in that noisome hole for a month when one morning a guard kicked open the cellar door and announced, with undisguised glee, that we were all being taken to Butirky prison.

It was the worst possible news, for Butirky was the place to which

Lubianka prisoners were sent to be executed, as it was in an area where the sound of shooting was less likely to cause any disturbance. (In the early days of the Revolution hundreds were reported to have been shot in a Lubianka 'execution cellar', perhaps the one where we had been held, while the engines of lorries were revved up outside the building to drown the gunfire.)

Soon after dawn, before most of the city was up and about, we were herded by armed guards and forced to walk five miles or so, through desolate streets and squares and out to Butirky, during which I developed a large and painful blister on my left foot. I asked to see the prison doctor, who turned out to be a real bitch in a white coat. After examining my foot, she told me, 'I am going to cut it open.' She lanced the blister without ceremony, and when I remarked that some disinfectant might not be out of place, she snapped back, 'What is the point of wasting good disinfectant? You are going to die, anyway.' As it happened, the foot did become infected and took some time to heal.

We shared one room at Butirky prison but it was much larger than the Lubianka cellar and we had camp beds to lie upon.

Unlike the Lubianka, there was no toilet available and all of us, men and women, had to make do with a line of buckets, which afforded no privacy. The only time we were allowed to move from the room was to slop out the buckets into the drains. Soon we became hardened to the disgusting routine.

We were all young and comparatively healthy, the oldest of us being in his thirties, and we were able to some extent to rise above the conditions. A gnawing hunger dominated our days, for the food we were given was barely sufficient to keep us alive. We tried to take our minds off our hunger by forming committees and having intellectual discussions on such topics as literature and philosophy, in fact anything except prison and our predicament.

Twice I was taken from the room for interrogation. The interrogator made no attempt to torture or in any way physically maltreat me. Instead he kept saying, 'You are a counter-revolutionary and you ought to be shot. Why did you join the people who are against us? After all, we are doing everything for the people and with the people. Give me one good reason why you are against us.'

Even though I knew it was but a few paces away from the firing squad I answered back with all the foolhardy impetuousness of youth. I told him I was very much in favour of the Revolution but I was just as strongly against the people who were implementing it. Warming to my theme, I said I could see no justification for thousands of people being shot merely because they did not share his views. He gave me a sour look and sent me back to join my fellow prisoners.

As the weeks went by the prospect of our release became less likely, and yet I was not afraid. It was not that I was brave, nor was I buoyed up by some inner religious conviction. In such situations – and this was confirmed by my experience in the Second World War – one develops a fatalistic attitude. You expect to be killed; you know there is nothing you can do about it, and yet you cannot imagine anyone will pull the trigger.

My release from Butirky came as the result of an incredible set of coincidences. Unknown to me, my father had been going round Moscow, exploring every means of gaining my freedom. He was at his wit's end when he met one of my mother's cousins, a woman who would have been cut dead by my mother in normal circumstances. This cousin had married beneath her social station to a tradesman, a Moscow locksmith, and the whole family felt she had let the side down. All this was forgotten when she saw the distraught state my father was in. 'Why, Herman,' she said. 'What on earth's wrong? You look so upset.' He told her, 'My son, Leopold, has been taken to Butirky gaol and you know what that means.'

She took his arm and said she might be able to help. By a supreme irony, the locksmith whom my mother despised so much had risen on the tide of the Revolution to a high position in the Cheka. Our cousin pressed her husband to intervene.

After more than three weeks in Butirky I was called into the office of the interrogator, who said, 'Young man, I am letting you go. You must be careful to behave yourself in future.'

I was flabbergasted and mystified, but I had learned my lesson. I assured him of my undying love for the Soviet regime and thanked him for his unbounded generosity. The next day I was free.

My father was waiting. He told me, with tears in his eyes, of our cousin's intervention and he repeated over and over that it was like a fairy tale come true. We went back to our lodgings and had a celebration dinner of boiled potatoes and yoghurt.

As far as I know, I was the only one released and all the others must have been executed or sent to Siberia. So many people disappeared the whole thing became impersonal, with each piece of sad news generating suitable noises and expressions of regret, but that was all. To dwell too long on the consequences of wars and revolutions would drive a person mad.

CHAPTER FIVE

Interned Again

Within days of my release from prison I went to Nizhni Novgorod with my father. I was welcomed like a prodigal son, but mother was in no mood for any more of my revolutionary nonsense. We were all going back to Riga, she said, and when mother made up her mind and used that tone of voice there was no room for argument. This time I could see there was more than a modicum of sense in what she proposed. The Baltic States of Latvia (formerly Livonia), Estonia and Lithuania had declared their independence and defended themselves against attacks by the German and Russian armies. In August 1920 Russia signed the Treaty of Riga, recognising Latvia as an independent State (treaties with Estonia and Lithuania had been signed earlier the same year). As a result, we could return to our homeland without hindrance.

Certainly we would be safer in Riga, where I and my brother and sister could resume our education and where our father had more chance of finding a source of income. We were classed as refugees and were put aboard one of the cattle truck trains with our pathetic bundles of personal property. The line ran through Moscow and on our arrival at the railway station there I was shocked to hear a loudspeaker announcement, 'Leopold Manderstam, report immediately to the Commandant of the Station.'

At the back of my mind for months had been the thought that the Red Army might seek me out as a deserter, in view of the way I had got out of the Army by fraudulent means. Had they caught up with me at last? There was also a fear that the Cheka had had second thoughts about my release from prison.

I was in a cold sweat as I walked to the Commandant's office and tapped timidly on the door. The uniformed official inside rose to his feet and greeted me with a beaming smile. To my great relief, he was an old school friend of mine, Nicolai Sinitzin.

'Thank God it's you!' I exclaimed.

He said he had seen my name on the passenger list and thought it would be nice to meet me again. Instead of detaining me, Nicolai shook me by the hand and wished me a safe journey.

I breathed much easier when, after four days in the capital, the train pulled out of Moscow with its load of Latvia-bound refugees. There was much confusion among the passengers about food and water supplies and other arrangements on which decisions had to be taken. The refugees agreed, as I had a soldierly appearance and was young and assertive, that I should take over. They elected me 'commandant of the train'.

It took us about a fortnight to reach Latvia during which time, as commandant, my duties included checks to make sure the rations were distributed fairly and that passengers' papers were in order. I also made a roll call every morning. At each of the stops we obtained hot water to make tea, but food was in very short supply.

When we arrived on the Latvian side of the border I faced a new crisis. The border guards demanded to know who was the commandant of the train and they took me to an interrogation centre, where I was accused of being a Communist. The wheel had turned full circle! My protestations of innocence were brushed aside. I must be a Communist or I would not have been made commandant of the train, they insisted. And after the recent fighting against the Russians they did not want any Bolshevik spies in Latvia.

The Latvians had set up a reception camp just inside the border, where they processed refugees and weeded out the undesirables, of whom I was regarded as a prime example. They even accused me of belonging to the Russian secret police. 'You are a member of the Cheka,' asserted the Latvian official. 'Even if you are not, you must have their permission and support or you would not have been allowed to take charge of the train.'

I tried to keep my temper, quietly telling the officials about my Latvian background and of my hatred for the Communists, while my family remained in the camp to support the statements I gave. It was a strange situation. I was not, strictly speaking, under arrest but confined to the camp area with orders to report to the office every morning. I was detained for three weeks and then, without explanation, the officials allowed me to leave, having been convinced by our statements or, more likely, after receiving word from Riga that we were telling the truth. We did not know what to expect in Riga but, by a stroke of luck, the owner of the apartment where we had lived before the war offered us our former home to rent. It was wonderful to be able to relax in comfortable, civilised surroundings once again and to pick up the threads of our lives.

It did not take long for father to build up his business contacts. After a while my sister left us to study at the University of Jena, Germany. I secured a place at the University of Riga, where most of the professors and tutors were German and where the emphasis was on German methods, an advantage for me because German was my mother's natural tongue and we all spoke that language at home. It was not so easy for other students to accept the state of affairs, since Latvia's regaining of independence had created a big upsurge in nationalism. Memories of the German occupation were still fresh in Latvian's minds, and student groups wanted only Latvian to be spoken, frowning upon anyone who was not 'pure Latvian'. I was born there, yet they still regarded me as an outsider. That was why my sister went to a German university. She took a medical degree and if she had stayed in Riga she would have had to use Latvian for the examinations, which would have been difficult for her. As I was in the science faculty, taking chemical engineering, the problem did not arise in my case. Not that I was an engineer by inclination. I dislike anything which involves an exact science, perhaps because I'm a romantic by nature.

Chemical engineering, however, appeared to offer me the easiest passage through university, and I obtained my Master's degree in fairly quick time, three-and-a-half years. It would have taken longer if the Latvian nationalist students had had their way. In my early days at university they went on strike against non-Latvians and set up picket lines across the entrance gates. Always a rebel, I was not going to allow them to stop me. I armed myself with a hefty stick and beat my way through the picket lines to attend lectures. Paradoxically, I learned little at university, simply because I had a very retentive memory and I could spout, parrot fashion, almost everything the professors said. When it came to examinations I used to repeat verbatim what the professors had told me. This made me appear brilliant, especially in the oral examinations, and it pleased the professors. 'My God,' I heard one of them say, 'the lad must have listened very carefully. He's taken note of my every word.' But this accumulation of facts and statements – whether on glassmaking, textiles, or whatever subject – was not knowledge I built upon. It did not increase my understanding of the subjects.

We 'foreigners' at the university formed our own society, of which I became the chairman. Our members comprised all the students who felt they were oppressed by the ultra-nationalist lobby, and the majority had either come from Russia as refugees or were of German extraction. It was at a meeting of the society that I was introduced to a girl who became my first wife. She was a Latvian, from Riga, and my parents were horrified when I took her home because her father was a plumber, a person whom my mother held in contempt. Of course, my own father earned his money from trade, but he was a *successful* businessman, a position mother could tolerate, even if she did not approve.

During my student days I was extremely shy as far as girls were concerned, even though I might have been overbearing in my relationships with other young men. I did not dance, I did not drink, I lacked the courage to ask girls out for dates, and I envied the suave young womanisers who danced into the early hours and who bragged about their conquests. Instead I tried to impress the ladies with my intellectual attainments. I read Dostoevsky, Tolstoy, Pushkin and Gogol from cover to cover, but few of my potential girlfriends were impressed when I quoted slabs of heavy literature at them.

I was a well-built, good looking youngster and there were occasions when I came close to losing my virginity, despite my bashfulness.

One of these occasions, when I was seventeen, involved the Polish daughter of a railway stationmaster. She was pretty, even though she had a cataract on her left eye. We went to a cinema once or twice and then came an evening when she invited me back to her home, adding with a sly smile, 'My parents will be out.' Inside the house, she took my hand and snuggled close. There was the usual fumbling, during which I became hot and bothered as she made it clear she was mine for the taking. Panic stations. I couldn't go through with it. Completely flustered, I scrambled to my feet and ran to the door, only to find the randy madam had locked it and removed the key. She watched in astonishment as I dashed across the room again, opened a window and dived into the night. The last train had long since departed and I had a six-mile walk in front of me. I was well on the way when I realised I'd left my hat behind, but I didn't go back for it.

That incident epitomises most of my relationships with women. I was not forever climbing through windows, except in the metaphorical sense, but I did not always have the guts to refuse an invitation. Thus I was caught up in involvements I did not want. The idea, the physical attraction, had very strong appeal and yet I could not cope with the emotional entanglements.

After I met my first wife, Helga, it was she who made all the running. We went for walks through Woehrmann Park and along the banks of the Western Dvina river, holding hands and dallying in the way courting couples do. Towards the end of one of these walks I gave her a passionate kiss. The next day her father turned up and said, 'I'm so glad you are going to be my son-in-law.' What is more he handed me a gold watch as an engagement present. I was trapped and there was no window to jump through. It took me six months to gather enough courage to tell my mother, and only then because the wedding was imminent. Poor mother. For a day or two she walked around in a stupor, murmuring, 'That my son should marry a tradesman's daughter . . .'

CHAPTER SIX

Working in South Africa

My horizons were broadened while I was at university. I travelled to Germany several times to see my sister, and I read medicine alongside her for two terms at Jena. Later on, I studied higher mathematics at the Sorbonne, which was really an excuse for me to stay in Paris. For the first two weeks of my student days in Paris, however, I was literally starving and I had no money to buy food. The only casual work I could find was a job no Frenchman would do, rolling barrels full of sulphuric acid on to lorries. If a barrel had burst there would have been no escape.

The job was an hour's travelling time from my lodgings and I had to get up at 5 am each day. With the first franc I earned I treated myself to a street kitchen meal of a bowl of soup, a slice of horsemeat and a piece of bread. No dinner at the Ritz could have tasted as good.

Helga stayed behind while I was engaged on these scholastic peregrinations. But there came a time when I realised I must find a more settled existence and a career.

My father had excited my imagination with tales of South Africa and of the opportunities it provided for someone who was young, fit and hard-working. Some of my wife's relatives also lived there.

So, in 1926, Helga and I sailed for Cape Town aboard the *Edinburgh Castle*. In the whole world there can be no more spectacular land fall than the approach to Cape Town. The long voyage from Europe had increased our anticipation and our first sighting of Table Mountain was a tremendous experience. As we moved into the bay, the mass of rock seemed to rise higher and higher, like a gigantic wall behind which lay the African continent. We were quite close before our attention was caught by the city nestling beneath the mountain.

Despite its attractions we did not stay long in Cape Town but took a train to Johannesburg, which in less than a lifetime had grown from a drab mining camp into a thriving city. I had accepted the offer of a job from my wife's uncle, Sam Gavronsky, at his Alberton soap and chemicals factory, about twenty miles outside Johannesburg.

Gavronsky was a stockily-built Jewish entrepreneur who had emigrated to South Africa twenty years earlier, from Lithuania. While most of the European immigrants to that area were preoccupied with the quest for gold, Gavronsky and his brother, Oscar, saw that the boom in population offered other openings for profit. They both made fortunes in the meat business and, like my father, they also dealt in leather and hides. Sam Gavronsky made his mark in another way, as the father of Helen Suzman, the South African Progressive Party leader and lifelong campaigner against apartheid, who was a leggy ten-year-old when I arrived in Johannesburg.

I was prepared to work hard for Gavronsky but he seemed to regard me as slave labour, and all for a miserable pittance of a salary. My routine was to get up at 6 am, ride to the factory on my trusty Harley Davidson motorbike, and work for between twelve and fourteen hours each day. I had an idea for recovering glycerine from soap and I worked many extra hours setting up the equipment and developing the project, for the benefit of my employer. This, I felt, deserved some compensation and I was upset when my modest claim for overtime pay was rejected, after I had completed a forty-eight hours stretch at the factory without going home. My employer angered me further by suggesting I had created the project merely as a means of getting overtime payments. That was the last straw. Without saying another word, I stalked out of his office, slamming the door on the way.

Next morning he sent a chauffeur-driven car to collect me from home.

'Let's forget about it,' he told me, by way of half-hearted apology. 'Everybody knows I've got a short temper.'

I was in no mood to be mollified and I walked out on him again, this time permanently.

It did not take me long to find another job in the Johannesburg area, with the Germiston Soap and Oil Company, which kept the wolf from the door for some months. Then I learned of a Portuguese-owned oil extraction plant across the border in Lourenço Marques, Portuguese East Africa, where a man with my particular skills was needed. The position seemed right down my street and the monthly salary of £100 in gold was excellent. I saw it also as an opportunity for me to show Gavronsky I was capable of getting much better-paid work than he could offer, and without the help of friends and relations. By that time my marriage to Helga had hit rough water and she stayed behind in Johannesburg.

Of course I had heard stories that Portuguese East Africa (Mozambique) could be a veritable 'white man's grave', but I chose to disregard them. Instead I felt some affinity with the early explorers, who saw East Africa as an El Dorado.

My journey from Johannesburg, through the Lebombo Mountains, was breathtaking. There was, however, a great contrast between the healthy air of the uplands and the malaria-laden mangrove swamps of the southern Mozambique coast; although Lourenço Marques itself, with golden sands facing the Indian Ocean and set amid the glorious colour of the tropics, was undergoing a transition into a pleasure resort for South Africans.

Unfortunately, I saw little of the colony's happier side. It was the rainy season when I arrived and I had a further disappointment when I found that my new boss, P. Santos Gil, was almost as much a slave driver as my first employer in South Africa and wanted more than full value for his money. I ran the factory for him and he expected me to be on call at all hours of the day and night. About the only relaxation I had was big game hunting, with leopards as the main prey because they were so abundant. I also went into the Kruger Game Reserve, where one was allowed to carry a rifle for self-defence, on condition that a seal was placed on the trigger, which was checked by a game warden at the end of each trip.

The factory had large stocks of highly flammable copra, kept in wooden store-sheds and one night these caught fire. I managed to get the blaze under control, using extinguishers, but my hands were badly burned in the process. Far from rushing to thank me, my employer did not visit me in hospital and when I was discharged, with my hands heavily bandaged, he gave me a very grudging welcome. Later on, I learned that the company had financial troubles and a fire insurance claim had seemed an easy way to get some cash.

After I had spent two years in Lourenço Marques, Santos Gil asked me to go to Europe on his behalf, to buy factory equipment. He did all his dealings in gold, and he packed a thousand gold sovereigns into a money belt. I tried not to appear conspicuous as I walked up the liner's gangplank with the gold strapped around my middle. On board the ship, heading for Durban, our first port of call, I felt decidedly groggy. A doctor came to the cabin to see me.

'I'm just seasick,' I told him.

'Like hell you are!' he exclaimed, 'You've got malaria.'

Those were the last words I heard until I came round in a Durban hospital. A nurse was bending over me, smiling, and she said, 'Don't worry. We have your belt.'

When I was well enough I completed my mission to Europe and returned to Lourenço Marques. I was put on my mettle by the arrival of an important visitor, Dr Samuel Evans, a mining magnate, who wanted to see the factory. It was part of my job to make sure everything was running as efficiently as a battleship. This I had done, but still I could not sleep. At two o'clock in the morning I drove over to the factory, just to satisfy myself all was well on the night shift. I had been there for two hours when, to my surprise, in walked Santos Gil and Dr Evans, who had been to a casino after a late dinner. A couple of days later I received a telephone call from Dr Evans, inviting me to see him at his hotel. He asked me to go to work for him, saying he had been impressed that I was still at the factory at 4 am and everything was so spick and span.

In 1932 I said farewell to Lourenço Marques, with few regrets, and went back to Johannesburg to supervise the building and fitting out of a factory for Dr Evans, which was to be run by his son. The Epic Oil Mill, as it was called, was similar to the Lourenço Marques factory and specialised in the extraction of oil from groundnuts, castor beans, sesame, sunflower seeds and copra.

I was regarded as an oddity, especially by black employees, because I supervised everything myself and was not afraid to roll up my sleeves and dive into the thick of the work. This was a practice I had started in my first job, at the Alberton soap factory, where I had sacked the foreman for drunkenness and had carried out his work until I found another foreman. At Alberton, and at Epic Oil, the blacks thought I was crazy. They said if they had a university education and were in my place they would sit behind a desk and let someone else do the work.

We had an accident while I was at Epic Oil, a big explosion in which four black employees were badly burned. I rushed to the scene with a first aid box and bandaged them up, an action regarded as *infra dig* by the Europeans. It was usual for European doctors to refuse to help a non-white, even if the person were dying. A native doctor had to be called. Such attitudes opened the door to Communist indoctrination. I had first hand experience of this in Lourenço Marques, when I employed a Zulu who had been trained by the Communists in Moscow. He had gone back to South Africa, where he fell into police hands and was roughly treated. After his release he crossed the border to Lourenço Marques and came to me for a job. He was an intelligent man, yet whenever he did anything wrong he would crouch on the floor in front of me and say, 'Boss, give me a kick.'

I refused to take part in such a ridiculous performance and he pleaded, 'You are my father, you are my brother, you are everything; therefore you must punish me. I would be much happier if you kicked me.'

We had an ominous meeting in my office shortly before I left Lourenço Marques, during which the Zulu said, 'Please, boss, don't settle in South Africa, for the time will come when everything white will be destroyed by us. We'll not leave even one white flower standing in the fields.'

His prophecy is bound to be realised. When one considers how the whites in South Africa are outnumbered seven times over then one is forced to conclude it's only a question of time. The problems will not be helped by the strategic importance of the Cape and the country's vast mineral wealth, which have long made South Africa a priority target for the Communists.

It is foolish to pretend the blacks are ready to take control of that beautiful, troubled land. Black South Africans, in my experience, instinctively give their strongest loyalties to individuals or small social groups and I cannot see them developing equally strong allegiances to the State, whether black or white, or to society in general.

Another complication is the gracious lifestyle which white people have built up over many generations, and the descendants of the early settlers believe they have a greater claim to their birthplace than do the more recent of the black and Asian immigrants. No white South African will be happy anywhere else, but there are dangers when attitudes become ingrained. One reason why I sent my daughter, Irene, to Europe was an incident when she was nine years old and we were sitting together, I reading the newspapers and she giggling her way through a pile of comics. She dropped one of the magazines on the floor and immediately summoned a servant from elsewhere in the house to pick it up. 'Oh, oh,' I said to myself. 'You're not going to carry on in that fashion, young lady, or you'll be very unhappy if ever you have to leave South Africa.' To her credit, she became a well-adjusted, caring woman; politically minded and with a great sense of humour.

*

The time I spent on Dr Evans's payroll in Johannesburg opened the way for an even better post, with a major international company, the General Mining and Finance Corporation. My years with General Mining were among the most stimulating and rewarding of my life. Once more I was given charge of a factory and, in all modesty, I must record that I made a success of it.

Perhaps the pinnacle of my career with General Mining came with my work on the conversion of castor oil into a more efficient lubricant. Castor oil was in universal use as a lubricant for rotary engines. But it had drawbacks, the most important of which was carbonisation at high temperatures. This tendency to 'gumming up' had plagued the operators of engines for years. If it could be overcome the advantages would be enormous, and not least in relation to aircraft engines. I was well aware of the implication in those pre-war, pre-jet days and tremendously excited when, after numerous laboratory experiments, I achieved a breakthrough.

I gave a full report to the head of General Mining, Sir George Albu, the son of the company's founder and who had taken control on his father's death in 1935. Sir George, about the same age as myself, became very enthusiastic about my invention. I was sent to

London in 1938 to test the oil conversion method with Professor Bolton, a great authority on the subject. He supported my findings and we established a pilot plant at Addlestone, in Surrey, which effectively proved that the operation could be a commercial success.

General Mining formed a subsidiary company to market the oil, with a million pounds capital, and Sir George offered me the managing directorship. I was riding on the crest of a wave. Of course, it could not last, but I wasn't prepared for the bombshell. Early in 1939, Sir George telephoned me and said, 'Sorry, Mandy. I've decided not to go ahead. There will be some compensation for you.' He sent me a cheque for £15,000, an enormous sum at the time, yet it did not remove the bitter taste. I seached for an explanation and the most logical one was that the oil companies had put irresistible pressure on Sir George. South African mines were big users of castor oil for lubricating their machinery and I knew the oil companies were afraid we would take all their business with our new process. Also they did not want to be forced to buy our oil to re-sell to their customers. As General Mining owned the patent and the commercial rights, there was nothing I could do about it.

For the next few months I was working from London on various industrial projects for General Mining. Sir George Albu took me with him twice to Rumania, where we operated the Phoenix Refinery in the Ploesti oilfields, which were later taken by the Germans and bombed by the Americans. My role on these trips was to make reports on the refinery operations, with a view to improving production. I was on the point of returning to South Africa when Germany invaded Poland and war was declared.

CHAPTER SEVEN

My Secret War

Soor after the outbreak of war I went to see the South African military adviser in London, General van der Spuy. I pointed out to him that I held a South African passport and I was officially in the country's Defence Force as a part-time soldier, Therefore, would he please send me back to join the South African Army?

'Hold your horses,' said the general, who was a veteran of the First World War. 'You're not going anywhere. As an engineer, you're in a reserved occupation and far more use here than in the Army.' Furthermore, he promised to put every obstacle in my way if I tried to leave General Mining.

I took the Tube back to our office in Winchester House, Old Broad Street. This was the British headquarters of General Mining's subsidiary company, Castor Oil Products, for which I was then working and whose board included W. W. Wakefield, the former England rugby captain. He was a good friend of mine, but he also poured cold water on my efforts to join the armed forces. 'You are staying here,' he snapped when I broached the subject. Usually one did not argue with Wakefield. He was big man in every sense, with shoulders like a buffalo and he walked with his head thrust forward, as if he were emerging with the ball from a loose scrum. His attitude towards me seemed unfair. He was an engineer himself and had not only served as a pilot in the 1914-18 war but had been recalled for flying duties in 1939. In fact he was so proud of his service that he attended the House of Commons in the uniform of a flight lieutenant when he was MP for Swindon.

In 1940 Wakefield was given a post at the Air Ministry and I was more determined than ever to join the forces, although I had temporarily switched my allegiance from the Army to the RAF. Eventually I was given an appointment to go before a selection board. I was accepted as a pilot officer, Intelligence, and was happily going down the steps to the street, clutching a voucher for a uniform, when who should I meet but 'W.W.' He stopped me in my tracks.

'Hello, Mandy,' he said. 'What the blazes are you doing here?' After I had explained, he called me all the silly fools under the sun. 'Do you realise what you will be doing?' he demanded. 'They'll send you to Scotland, where you will be a glorified clerk, taking down reports from pilots. A good engineer will be wasted. You are not going to get a commission – I'll see to that!'

Somewhat deflated, I walked away, uncertain whether or not he could carry out his threat. After all, I did have my little piece of paper. My hopes were dashed completely when I received a terribly nice letter from the Air Ministry, expressing regret and advising me that my commission had been suspended 'until further orders'. I really saw red and marched round to Wakefield's office, burst in and told him precisely what I thought of him. 'You stopped my commission,' I yelled. 'Well, you might prevent me getting into the RAF but you won't stop me joining the Army.'

'Wait, Mandy,' he said, in his best placatory manner. 'Do you really mean that? Are you so determined to get in?'

'Yes, I am,' I told him. 'I'm going across the road to the Recruiting Office and I shall join the Army as a private, as Mr Brown, or Mr Smith, or Mr Finklestein. You won't stop me.'

He smiled. 'All right, Mandy. Don't do anything yet. Just give me a few days.'

I heard no more until a long buff-coloured envelope dropped on to my hall mat with a mysterious letter from the War Office, Room 055, saying would I please report next day at 10 am. Nothing else. Naturally, I did as I was told and was interviewed by Colonel Anthony Benham. We went through the necessary preliminaries and inquiries about my background, the countries I had lived in, my knowledge of languages, my views on the war and how I might be able to help. Colonel Benham was apparently satisfied with the answers, for he asked me if I was interested in joining an outfit called Special Operations Executive. He said SOE was a clandestine organisation, the training was tough and the work involved great risks.

'You would be on your own and should anything go wrong we

would not be able to help you, nor would we acknowledge your existence,' he explained.

I was not naive enough to see myself as a latter-day Richard Hannay, but I was excited at the prospect of getting into the war at last. The next step was to attend an interview at 64 Baker Street, the SOE headquarters, where I was ordered to report to Arisaig, Inverness, for training.

After the delays and rejections of the previous months it was exhilarating to find events moving so swiftly. It was obvious Wakefield had pulled a few strings, yet I was baffled by the ease with which I had passed the vetting procedure. Later I learned that Wakefield had spoken about me to Dr Hugh Dalton, the Minister of Economic Warfare, who was responsible for SOE. Dalton was intrigued by my Russian upbringing and also by my knowledge of Germany. He did not appear to know I had been in the Red Army and I did not tell him, although I did mention the fact to a security officer, who apparently disregarded the information after telling me, 'We'll not talk about that.' The factor which tipped the balance heavily in my favour was the time I had spent in Africa, an area of weakness as far as the British secret services were concerned.

SOE came into being during July 1940, a month after Dunkirk, with orders from Churchill to create chaos with actions of subversion and sabotage. The organisation took over a role that had previously been the responsibility of several departments. It made up the rules as it went along and was loathed in the upper echelons of the Foreign Office, who looked upon SOE as beyond the pale; rather as a maiden aunt might regard a niece who had become a successful callgirl.

The Foreign Office, rulers of Britain's secret services for generations, preferred to operate in less direct ways. I called them 'the spooky boys'. But we were spooky boys, too. We had to bury our identities and live the roles we had been given. Not even asleep must we forget our lines, for a wrong word on waking up could betray oneself, and possibly betray comrades as well.

A basic difference between us and the uniformed combatants was that the danger to us increased a hundredfold if we were captured, whereas a uniformed soldier who became a prisoner could plead the Geneva Convention and, if he wished, could sit tight in comparative safety, waiting for the liberation. There were exceptions, particularly in the Far East, but generally speaking a uniformed combatant who had faced bullets, shells and bombs was no longer in danger of his life once he was behind barbed wire.

A captured agent, on the other hand, faced at best a concentration camp and the near certainty of execution. And death might come as a blessed release after the cruel refinements of interrogation practised by the Gestapo. Another difference I found most striking was that a high proportion of SOE's 'front line troops' were women, the bravest of the brave.

I never did find out whether the SOE address had been chosen by a Sherlock Holmes fan with a sense of humour or whether it was just a coincidence. As is well known now, we were dubbed The Baker Street Irregulars. It was an apt title, although I was not familiar with it. We were more likely to refer to The Racket, or The Firm. Throughout the war The Racket occupied several buildings in the Baker Street area. Of course, no plaques advertised its presence, save for a bland Inter-Services Research Bureau plate on a wall, designed to explain the comings and goings to any curious passer-by. Infinite pains were taken to protect the secrecy of SOE. Its operational chief, Major-General Sir Colin Gubbins (he was then a brigadier) was known by the symbol M, and it was not until well after the war that the public learned of his existence and of the vital work which he directed. He was a veteran of the 1914-18 war, having served in France and Belgium. He also spent six months in Archangel as ADC to Lord Ironside.

Colin Gubbins had developed an interest in underground warfare when he was posted to Ireland in the 1920s. He went to Warsaw as an Intelligence officer and escaped Hitler's invasion of Poland literally with hours to spare. Next he was recruited to MI(R), which preceded SOE and under whose aegis the various elements of irregular warfare were gathered. In 1940 he was chosen to organise 'striking companies' as part of the British Expeditionary Force in Norway, gaining valuable first hand experience in sabotage. Winston Churchill had a high regard for Gubbins and personally named him as the man to organise Britain's resistance movement if Hitler's invasion forces crossed the Channel.

With that background, Gubbins was tailor-made for SOE.

Behind the brisk, no-nonsense military approach he presented to the
world was an intelligent, sensitive man; a great organiser who had
a highly developed sense of humour and a huge capacity for
friendship. Gubbins had to weld together as strange a mixture of
people as you could find, drawn from all over Europe and including
businessmen, lawyers, ex-convicts, shopgirls, secretaries, artists,
journalists and schoolmasters.

Among the first things Gubbins did when he took over as SOE
Director of Operations and Training was to set up Special Training
Schools. One of these was the place to which I was sent, Arisaig, or
STS No 26, in a really desolate and windswept part of the
Highlands.

The spot, in western Inverness-shire, had been selected by
Gubbins himself. There, on a course lasting six weeks, we learned
unarmed combat, how to kill quickly and silently, how to survive in
rough country, how to use a wide variety of weapons, how to plant
and detonate explosives – in short all the skills required of an
efficient saboteur. My training in chemistry and engineering gave
me a distinct advantage in the use of the comparatively new plastic
explosives.

The SOE hopefuls under training when I was at Arisaig were
mostly, like myself, well into their thirties and some were overfed
City gent types who were almost killed by the mountaineering and
survival exercises. We had arrived by train from Glasgow at seven
o'clock on a winter's morning, to be met by a trim young lieutenant
called Robinson, who announced, 'Well, gentlemen, before
breakfast we will have a little walk.' He then took us for an eight
miles slog through the frozen mountains. Breakfast was an inedible
concoction. In fact all the food was terrible. I preferred K rations,
a pack comprising a few raisins, a small bar of chocolate and a tin
of self-heating soup. (The tin contained a small quantity of
aluminium tri-oxide which ignited when a plug was pulled, exposing
it to the air.) We supplemented our food supplies by throwing hand
grenades into the loch to kill trout and roach, which we grilled over
wood fires.

The officers had a habit of waking us up around 2 am, to go for
training runs. They also sent a few of us into the frost and snow to
spend a night out of doors without any provisions. But we found a

snug little croft, where the crofter invited us to be his guests until morning. He gave us a hearty breakfast and refused point blank to accept any payment. I have had a soft spot for Scottish folk ever since.

The commanding officer at Arisaig was a Colonel Evans. His training officer was Major Sykes, a marvellous shot, who came to SOE from the Shanghai Police. Sykes looked and spoke like a bishop, very quiet and mild. In his lectures he would say the most gruesome things in his soft bishop's voice.

'During unarmed combat, if you get the chance, insert a finger into a corner of your opponent's mouth and tear it. You will find the mouth tears very easily . . .' And after describing particularly vicious ways of crippling and disarming an enemy, he would often end with the remark, '. . . and then kick him in the testicles.'

Fortunately, I never had to use the fighting skills I was taught at Arisaig but it did make me more confidant, knowing I could pull something out of the hat if I faced an aggressive foe in hand-to-hand combat. The Arisaig CO, in his report, assessed me as 'first class', which I did not deserve and which I attributed to the probability that he was drunk when he wrote it. I also collected top marks from the second phase of the training programme, an initiative test carried out in Manchester, in which luck played the most important part. We were each given an assignment during which we must act precisely as if we were active agents in the field. A War Office telephone number was issued to us, to be divulged only as a last resort, if we were arrested and could not bluff ourselves out of custody. The instructing officer said the local police had been given my description, with the warning that I was a German spy. Then he came to my assignment: to steal the plans of the Manchester Oil Refinery. For anyone else it would have seemed an extremely tough proposition. But when he told me I restrained a hoot of laughter with great difficulty – my firm had built the refinery!

I walked out of the office, telephoned Francis Kind, a friend of mine who was the refinery manager, and arranged to see him. He sent a Rolls-Royce to meet my train and to convey me to the refinery. 'I need the plans because we're making contingency preparations in case of bombing,' I told Francis, and he gave me all I needed. My instructors were impressed by the speed and efficiency with which

I fulfilled the assignment. While I was at Manchester I also completed my parachute training with nine jumps over Ringway Airfield.

My appointment to SOE was confirmed and to this day the records held by the Ministry of Defence show I was 'Appointed . . . without pay and allowances from Army Records for duties with the Inter-Services Research Bureau.' Such is the mystery surrounding SOE that the list of postings and promotions is full of mistakes. The surviving records kept by the Foreign Office are more specific but they also contain inaccuracies, and contradict those held at the Ministry of Defence. That is hardly surprising. So much of SOE's work was not officially recorded and a great deal of material relating to our activities was deliberately destroyed.

On my return to Baker Street I was given a desk and the rank of captain in the General List. I dashed over to Buckingham Palace in my new uniform, with its gleaming Sam Browne belt, for the pleasure of watching the Royal sentries salute me, or rather my uniform.

I remained at Baker Street for the early months of 1941, kicking my heels as a member of the chairborne brigade and I almost despaired of seeing any action. My hopes rose when I received a message from Tony Benham, saying Julius Hanau wanted to see me. Hanau, inevitably known as Caesar, was an energetic but dry and inscrutable man. He had worked for Section D, whose operations included neutral countries and was later put in charge of SOE's West Africa desk in London. Given the choice, I would have volunteered for a parachute drop into France, or even Germany. That was not the way SOE worked, however. We rarely had a choice.

'Manderstam, do you know Portuguese West Africa?' began Hanau, confirming my worst fears with his first sentence.

'No, sir.'

'I see. Well, can you speak Portuguese?'

'No, sir,' I lied again, less confidently.

'Umm . . . pity. Have you any familiarity with the Portuguese way of life?'

This time my denial sounded even more shaky. The suspicion

dawned on me that security, despite its chronic incompetence, had unearthed the details of my two years in Lourenço Marques, which I had not divulged.

Unperturbed, Hanau went on, 'I have called you here to inform you that you have been chosen for an operational assignment. Here is your Movement Order.' He shoved a document across the desk.

'You are leaving tomorrow for Luanda, via Lagos, as part of our West African Section. Your code will be W20. Your chief objective will be to get possession for Britain of a Vichy ship, the *Gazcon*, now lying in the neutral waters of Lobito harbour. I must warn you the SIS have already tried to persuade the captain to abandon his ship, without success. I hope you have better luck. Anyway, see what you can do.'

Before picking up the details of my travelling arrangements from Benham, I called at the Security Office, where a normally effusive Irish officer called Jack O'Reilly, a former Special Branch policeman, was waiting to give me a final briefing. For once, O'Reilly was in no mood for small talk. He said he could give me half an hour and he would not repeat himself, so I should listen carefully. He impressed on me the need for secrecy. Not even my family should be given any hint about my destination or the nature of my mission. All my kit must be surrendered, unmarked, to the Security staff, so they could ensure it bore no indication of my identity or of my destination. Any letters or packets which I sent, or received, would be despatched in Diplomatic Bags and inspected by Security before delivery. Absolute secrecy must be maintained, O'Reilly repeated.

The following morning I arrived at Euston Station in civilian clothes, as instructed, and I looked around in vain for a Transport Officer, to whom I could report my arrival. I scanned the platform for a friendly face, and my attention was caught by an all too familiar object. It was my kitbag, lying unattended by the ticket barrier and bearing a label which announced in glaring Army block letters:

CAPTAIN MANDERSTAM
DESTINATION GREENOCK

CHAPTER EIGHT

Atlantic Alert

On the train, heading northwards to Greenock, I met up with Captains Lippett and Long and three other members of the West African Section. We were all scheduled to board a Merchant Navy ship, the *John Holt*, at the Scottish port and to proceed to Takoradi, in what was then the British colony of The Gold Coast.

At Greenock we found amid our unloaded luggage a large and extremely heavy suitcase, which was assigned to Captain Lippett. He had been ordered not to let it out of his sight. The old case was clearly feeling the strain of years of battering from porters and, to our consternation as Lippett was carrying it on to the ship it burst open, spilling on to the gangplank and into the harbour a stream of ammunition, firearms, hand-grenades and explosives. We gathered up what we could of our 'equipment' and carried it aboard, a little shamefaced, as the crew watched. No questions were asked, although the sailors must have wondered what a gang of obviously incompetent amateurs were doing on board their ship. The magic word 'security' worked its spell.

We left Greenock in mid-June, as part of a convoy of eighteen merchant ships with an escort of two destroyers. In this gallant company we felt safe as houses. The weather was fine and only the smallest waves disturbed the surface of the sea as we steamed majestically into the North Atlantic. The calm sea was a mercy for me, as I was never a good sailor, and for one of the few times in my life I could enjoy a stroll on deck.

Two days out from Greenock we had our first piece of excitement when the escort ships picked up sonar signals from suspected German submarines. Immediately the destroyers went into concerted action. They swept in giant circles around the convoy, like mother ducks guarding their young. Every two hundred yards they fired depth charges, which brought up bubbling eruptions of foam.

Petersburg-Moscow
press, on which
anderstam travelled.

biansky Square, Moscow,
ough which Manderstam
s taken to prison.

nni Novgorod. Centre can
seen the outline of the
dge of boats.

Trotsky.   Kerensky.

Porte Iverskia, Moscow, at the time that L. H . Manderstam was in the city.

From the bosom of the convoy we watched this operation with equanimity. The two destroyers continued the encircling manoeuvre for the rest of the day and throughout the night and the following day. At the end of the third day at sea the destroyers turned, signalled 'good luck', and headed back in the direction of the British coast. The Royal Navy could no longer spare them.

With their departure, the situation changed dramatically and the sea took on a much more threatening aspect. The *John Holt* was an ordinary merchant ship of the West African Holt Line. Its only defence was a three-inch gun and a detachment of Army gunners. Capable of bringing down a few seagulls, I thought, but not much good in a real emergency. Our apprehension increased when we received a warning that a German U-boat was in the area.

In such circumstances it was usual for unprotected merchant convoys to scatter. This allowed the captain of the *John Holt* to take advantage of his superior speed and, cruising at twenty knots, we cut a long swerving course across the Atlantic towards Newfoundland and back round the Azores, minimising the threat from submarine attack. The more direct route was too close to the German re-fuelling stations in France and on the African coast.

We had no sonar, of course, and had to rely entirely on the sharpness of our eyes. Each of us took a four-hour turn on watch.

When it came to my stint I could not take it seriously and I just sat on deck, day-dreaming and whistling. The sailors were upset and explained that whistling was a nautical taboo. They believed bad luck would follow. I wondered if there might be something in their superstition when, on a subsequent watch, I saw a dark speck where formerly there had been only water. The speck appeared to be no bigger than a squashed gnat on a wet windscreen and it was hard to make out against the sparkle of the waves. I screwed up my eyes. It began to look very much like a submarine periscope. Not that I had seen a periscope in real life, but I had seen them on films, poking from the water like serpents' heads. I sent word to the captain, who confirmed my diagnosis. He could not say whether it was a German or friendly submarine and there was no point in staying to find out. The *John Holt*'s engines were turned to full speed ahead and we swung into a series of sharp zig-zags. We saw no more of the submarine, but I was a good deal more alert during my watches from that moment.

For most of the time, we were bored out of our minds by the inactivity, the throbbing engines and the seemingly limitless ocean. I suppose the same was true of the majority of long sea voyages during the war. We searched for ways to relieve the tedium and The Affair of the Vanished Pistol gave us an opportunity. After two weeks at sea, Captain Lippett, announced that a pistol was missing and he wanted to know where it had gone. My reaction was to say the gun had obviously been nicked by someone on the ship and it did not matter.

Lippett was aghast. He was a stickler for protocol.

'Matter?' he barked. 'Of course it matters. In the Army things do not just vanish into thin air. They are "lost in action" or "captured by the enemy". They are not allowed simply to disappear.'

So what could we do? 'I think we need a Court of Enquiry.' said Lippett, in a magisterial tone. He would be the investigator/ prosecutor, Captain Long would be the Clerk of Court, three other officers would form the jury. And who would preside over this court? 'Oh, you will be the judge,' Lippett informed me.

He seemed to know what he was doing, so the rest of us let him get on with his arrangements. I was gratified to hear the court proceedings did not need to begin at once. First there had to be a preliminary investigation, which in effect meant spreading word around the ship, asking either for information about the pistol or its return. We waited several days but there was no response from the crew.

Accordingly, at 1100 hours on a windy Atlantic day six of us foregathered, in uniforms, in the cabin of the investigator and the judge, alias Lippett and myself. This done, I waited further help from Lippett, but he appeared to be at a loss for words, a most unusual phenomenon as far as he was concerned. The Clerk of the Court came to the rescue. 'Couldn't you start by asking what were the results of the investigation?' he suggested.

'Good idea,' snapped Lippett.

'All right,' I said, 'What has the investigation revealed?'

'Nothing,' replied Lippett.

'Then what the bloody hell do you think happened to it?'

Lippett was taken aback by this direct, if somewhat improper line of questioning from the judge.

'Oh, I suppose someone pinched it,' he said lamely.

'And who do you think it was?'

'Person unknown,' he replied, recovering his composure.

This seemed to conclude the proceedings and Long, our Clerk of Court, rose quietly and was sneaking out of the door.

'Not so fast,' Lippett called after him. 'Your job is not finished. Take this down: "The Court finds, in the light of all available evidence, that the missing article herein described has been purloined by a person unknown."'

I quickly declared the case closed and suggested we should adjourn for lunch, which was not an attractive proposition.

Because of our attempts to avoid the German submarines we had been at sea for double the estimated duration of the voyage, and our food supplies were running low. The captain had put us all on emergency rations of corned beef and dry biscuits. I went to see the purser and asked if he had received many complaints about the food.

'Complaints?', he howled. 'Have I had complaints? I can tell you, Captain Manderstam, I've had those blighters up to *here*.' He delivered a mock karate chop to his gullet. 'Rations is rations, and I can't change them.'

Perhaps not, I agreed, but he could change the menu. So we devised a new menu, starting with Beluga caviar on toast, followed by a choice of Scotch salmon or lobster mayonnaise and rounded off with strawberry meringue and *crème brulée*. This was elaborately printed and distributed. The purser was bombarded with questions. It was a special 'farewell dinner' which Captain Manderstam had been saving for them as a surprise, he said, ignoring the fact that we were still at least a week away from Takoradi.

As the dinner hour approached, I and five fellow officers settled at the table in full uniform. Excited voices mingled with the impatient tinkling of knives and forks. The galley door swung open; a steward marched in with a large tray on which two gleaming domes hid the food. The domes were lifted, revealing, to a barrage of invective, six slices of corned beef and six dry biscuits. If there had been a gangplank on the *John Holt* the purser and I would probably have walked it. With luck, however, the lads might have been laughing too hard to push us off.

Heading back across the Atlantic, we were still some days from the African coast when we encountered a British destroyer. Despite his misgivings, I persuaded the *John Holt*'s captain to send a signal to the destroyer saying he had officers on board who were delayed on an important mission. We requested the destroyer to take us aboard and deliver us to Takoradi. Back came a reply from the destroyer's commander, 'Who do you think you are? If there are any orders they will come from the Admiralty and not from you.' And he stormed away from us.

We reached Takoradi in mid-July and found it swarming with troops. Twenty thousand British soldiers and a Free French battalion were stationed there and the major topic of conversation was not the war effort but the prevalence of VD among the Britons. The French were virtually clear of VD and the explanation was not too difficult to find. The French, in their practical way, had set up properly supervised brothels, a facility denied to the Tommies because of the British Army's usual hypocritical approach to sexual matters.

From Takoradi I flew down the coast to Lagos on a DC3, the workhorse of our forces in Africa. Louis Franck, a Belgian, was in charge of operations in Lagos, where I stayed for three weeks. In peacetime Louis was a city gent, a leading bullion specialist, and he was cunning as a fox. Louis could find his way round almost any problem. I recall the ingenious method by which he avoided a ban on the export of bullion. All he did was to turn the ingots into Buddhas and send them to India, as there was no restriction on the export of *objêts d'art* made from gold.

We called him 'the blond bombshell', due to the colour of his hair and his reputation as a ladies' man. He was an extraordinary dresser, a little on the caddish side, and he caused pained expressions in some quarters by wearing suede shoes with his uniform. Gubbins was impressed by Louis's up-to-date knowledge of what was going on in Baker Street. We all knew the reason. As soon as he arrived from foreign parts, Louis took a Baker Street secretary out for a meal and found out all the latest news *before* he went to see Gubbins. Louis was, as they say, a smart operator.

When I arrived in Lagos Louis Franck was busy with Operation

Postmaster, a plan to capture two Italian ships from the neutral island of Fernando Po, Spanish Guinea. It was a mission similar to the one I had been asked to undertake, with a non-SOE team in charge of the scheme's naval element. So far as Operation Postmaster was concerned, I merely watched from the sidelines and I was joined by Hedley Vincent, who had also come out from London. (Hedley was later to strengthen my Angola section. He had served briefly as a gunner and in the Intelligence Corps before being caught up in SOE's net. His charming young wife, Sibyl, a civilian ambulance driver at the start of the war, followed us to Lagos. She had been recruited by SIS in a secretarial capacity but she later worked for SOE.)

Captain Lippett, who had accompanied me on the ship from Greenock, was sent over to Santa Isabel, Fernando Po, to prepare the ground for Operation Postmaster. According to the scheme worked out in Lagos, Lippett was to give a party ashore for the sailors and the port's Spanish officials while two British-manned tugs dashed into the harbour and towed the ships out to sea for a rendezvous with a cruiser. One of the tugs was grounded for a time and the operation looked likely to be completely messed up, although they did succeed in taking the Italian mixed cargo/passenger vessel *Duchessa D'Aosta*. The Spanish authorities were quick to see the ulterior motive behind the largesse so generously dispensed to the sailors by Lippett and they arrested him. He was given a rough time in police custody and was in poor shape when he was eventually released after strong representations. In my opinion he did not get the credit he deserved for his work on Operation Postmaster.

I was not around to see the aftermath of that episode, as I had to leave by air for Leopoldville. From Leopoldville I went by train to Matadi and I completed the last lap by car to Luanda, the Angolan capital. Luanda, once a major centre of the slave trade, was a busy deepwater port with a fine harbour protected by an eighteen miles long sandy island. Coffee, rubber, coconuts, sugar and tobacco flourished in the hot and moist climate, which reminded me of my time in Mozambique. There were other similarities in the two Portuguese colonies on either side of the African continent. And they were important to us in 1941 as neutral countries where we had official representatives and also secret agents who could keep watch on submarine and shipping movements in the Atlantic and Indian Oceans.

Supplies of essential goods flowed from the colonies. A strong Allied presence in West Africa was particularly vital because of the Benguela Railway, conveying freight from one coast to the other, thus enabling shipping to avoid the dangerous Cape route, where U-boats lurked on constant patrol.

My first duty in Luanda was to report to the British Consul-General, Victor Cusden, who told me his appointment gave him a rank equivalent to a major-general and he was entitled to a nineteen-gun salute. I must do nothing without his permission. Did I understand? I repeated, 'Yes, sir,' at regular intervals, privately thinking him a pompous little man. But when I got to know Cusden, I discovered he was playing a part, just as I was, the difference being that his strings were pulled by the Foreign Office. He was, in his natural self, anything but pompous – a well-mannered, friendly person, who put his career at risk more than once for the Allied cause. After listening to him for an hour, I promised to behave myself and said I fully realised he was in control and I must consult him before taking any action.

I was in Angola for little more than a week on that first trip before I was called back to London to report on what I had seen and heard. There had been difficulties, I believe, in getting clearance from the SIS for me to carry out the *Gazcon* plan.

It was 9 pm when I reached my flat in St. John's Wood and I telephoned Baker Street to tell them of my arrival. The only message for me was the news that I would probably have fourteen days' leave. I hardly had time to relish a piping hot bath and to settle in an armchair with a cup of coffee when the telephone rang. It was Benham. Report to Baker Street in the morning for briefing, he said. I was being sent straight back to Angola. This put a damper on my arrangements for a late dinner at Hatchett's Restaurant, followed by a long lie-in the next day.

'Don't be silly. I've only just got in. You can't do this to me,' I moaned.

'Oh yes we can. You're in the Army,' he said with a laugh and did not respond to my assertion that I was not in the Army but SOE.

A few days later I was in Gibraltar waiting for a ship, any ship, bound for West Africa. There was a Joint Intelligence Unit operating from Gibraltar, where reports from Army Intelligence, SIS and SOE were pooled. And while I was waiting I was sent over to Tangier by boat to find out what I could. (The Free Territory of Tangier had been annexed by Spain in May 1941.)

Gibraltar had been turned into a great fortress with miles of tunnels in the rock, some of them signposted with the names of London streets. Despite the constant threat of air attacks there was no problem about getting to and from Tangier. Apart from the clandestine links with North Africa, there was a regular boat service between Tangier and Algeciras, Spain, just across the bay from Gibraltar. Information which I obtained from our contact in Tangier, who was the head porter at the biggest hotel (I think it was the Minos) was passed to the Joint Intelligence Unit. It was impossible to tell how important these snippets were, being mostly about the arrival and departure of German and other VIPs, snatches of gossip and details of the activities of suspicious characters who were thought to be German agents. The bits and pieces were fitted together like a jigsaw by the Unit, or at least that was the theory.

Soon after I returned from Tangier I went to see the officer in charge of SOE's arrangements, as I recall a Colonel 'Tiger' Morris, fully expecting to be put aboard a Royal Navy destroyer. He must have liked a joke, for he told me, 'I've found you something, a boom defence vessel going to Hong Kong and it will be stopping at Lagos. Just the thing.'

I was flabbergasted. A walk down to the harbour confirmed my worst fears. The ship, if such it could be described, was small, no more than 160 tons, dirty and flat-bottomed, and it had two ugly horns sticking out, to pick up the harbour booms. The Transport Officer could not have found a vessel less suited to such a reluctant sailor as myself.

In a heated exchange of signals, I told the London office a British officer should not have to travel in these conditions, and I received the brusque reply that I would take the transport provided for me, and if I disobeyed orders I could be court-martialled.

The skipper of the ill-equipped tub earned my unstinting admiration for his guts in embarking on that long-way-round voyage to the Far East, with a crew of six. He was about sixty years of age, a North Country fisherman in peacetime, transformed by the war into a grease-stained RNVR sub-lieutenant.

We headed into the Atlantic, towards the Azores, avoiding the Vichy-held coast of North Africa. Three days out of Gibraltar, we saw two Spanish frigates approaching. They might just as well have been Germans, as our cocky little skipper was not well versed in the niceties of wartime pacts. He ordered us to 'action stations'. We turned our full armaments of two machine-guns and one three-inch gun in the direction of the frigates.

'We'll show the buggers,' muttered our captain, his eyes glinting with anticipation. And he was most upset when the frigates went on their way towards Spain without giving us a second glance. They did not think we were worth bothering about.

Somewhere off the coast of French Equatorial Africa the boom defence vessel's engines ground to a halt and we drifted helplessly in the Atlantic swell. The bearings on the propeller drive shaft had seized up and, following the skipper's example, we all rolled up our sleeves and spent several hours polishing the bearings and cleaning the shaft. Apparently this was an occupational hazard with the rusty hulk.

The engines took up their regular beat again and we resumed our normal shipboard duties, which for me included looking after one of the Hotchkiss machine guns. I had been working on the gun and was sitting beside it, looking aimlessly towards the horizon when I noticed an aircraft heading our way.

'Plane approaching!' I shouted.

We had no binoculars available to help us identify the aircraft, but our peppery old skipper did not wait for verification.

'Fire! I order you to fire! Shoot the bastard!'

I got the aircraft in my sights. By the grace of God the gun jammed, and as the aircraft swooped past I saw quite clearly American markings on its wings and fuselage. It had probably come from their Azores base.

I must have looked green around the gills and certainly I felt ill as a result of the vessel's disconcerting motion through the heavy sea.

'You look bloody awful, Mandy,' said our helpful skipper. 'I'll fix you up in no time.'

He went below and came back with a mug of hot water, condensed milk and chopped-up raw onion.

'Drink this. You'll feel better.'

If he wanted to cure my sickness by emptying my stomach he succeeded. It was, he maintained, an ancient remedy used by seamen. They swore by it, he said, to which I replied that I was not surprised.

There were no more mishaps before, at long last, we reached port and I travelled to Luanda by my former route.

CHAPTER NINE

Capture of the Gazcon

My business connections gave me an excellent cover while I was working in West Africa. As an employee of General Mining I had every reason to be there. Before my arrival, SOE did not have a mission in Angola and it was part of my job to establish one. First, however, I had to find a way of delivering into the care of the Royal Navy the Vichy merchant ship *Gazcon*, (4,224 tons), which was trapped in Lobito harbour by a shortage of fuel and the reluctance of the Portuguese to assist it on its way.

The ship and its cargo of chromium and timber were together valued at £406,000, a worthy prize and one which had already exercised the mind of the Foreign Office. My task was not made any easier by the fact that the SIS had been unable to win over Captain Briot, the ship's master.

In a confidential report, now lodged in the archives of the Service Historique de la Marine at Vincennes, Captain Briot stated that the *Gazcon* had left Tamatave, Madagascar, on 19 May 1941, for Dakar. The ship encountered bad weather and, as a result, did not have enough fuel to reach its destination. He said he put into neutral Lobito in mid-June, and it took two months of negotiations before the Portuguese authorities allowed him to take aboard six hundred tonnes of coal.

That was the situation when I came into the picture. My first priority was to gain Briot's confidence and, to that end, I contacted the Lobito harbourmaster, a man called da Costa, asking him to get me an introduction. Da Costa was in our pay, although I did not know who his paymaster was – possibly one of the SIS people. There was no problem, da Costa told me, and he arranged for me to see the captain within a matter of hours.

At our first meeting, Captain Briot was very much on his dignity, almost certainly because of the earlier hamfisted approaches to him.

'Do you realise you are dealing with a Frenchman, an officer and a gentleman?' he said, visibly swelling with pride inside his uniform.

'But *you* are dealing with someone who is neither an officer, nor a gentleman; nor, for that matter, even an Englishman,' I replied. 'In any case, I'm not trying to bribe you, I am offering you compensation for the risks involved.'

Every man has his price and I set Briot's at £10,000, which amounted to 40,000 dollars at the going exchange rate. He accepted the deal, but how was it to be accomplished? We put our heads together at that, and subsequent, hush-hush meetings. We had to be extremely careful in our negotiations because the *Gazcon* had a rabid Nazi as second-in-command. If any hint had leaked out he would have gone to any lengths to foil our scheme, possibly by reporting us to the Portuguese authorities, or by scuttling the ship.

Briot gave me a list of his crew members, pointing out that seven of them were anti-Vichy and would willingly join the Free French forces, if it could be arranged. The Foreign Office sent me an urgent message saying I *must* get permission from General de Gaulle himself before I enrolled the men. The FO was fearful of upsetting the great man. As it happened, de Gaulle was not far away, at Brazzaville, in the French Congo, so I set off to see him. He could be very stuffy and was rather sensitive about his position as a wartime leader, but his ADC, Colonel Allegret, was a friend of mine, who was an enormous help in setting up the meeting. I had got to know Allegret in Luanda. A delightful man, he came in with me when I saw de Gaulle. Allegret had a Czech wife, who liked to converse with me in Russian, and he assisted me with my rusty French.

De Gaulle listened to me in silence, and when it came to the request for his consent for me to recruit and arm the Frenchmen, he looked up and said simply, *'D'accord.'* The meeting was over. I had got his agreement and I hurried back to Luanda.

Briot's motivation was the bribe I had promised to pay, not patriotism, although he was by no means a Nazi. He arranged for me to see the seven anti-Vichy crewmen in the woods on the Lobito peninsula. I took along pistols for each of them, plus a couple of hand grenades. Under my instruction they practised with the guns and I showed the sailors how to take them to pieces. It would be their duty, I told them, to kill the Nazi second-in-command should that

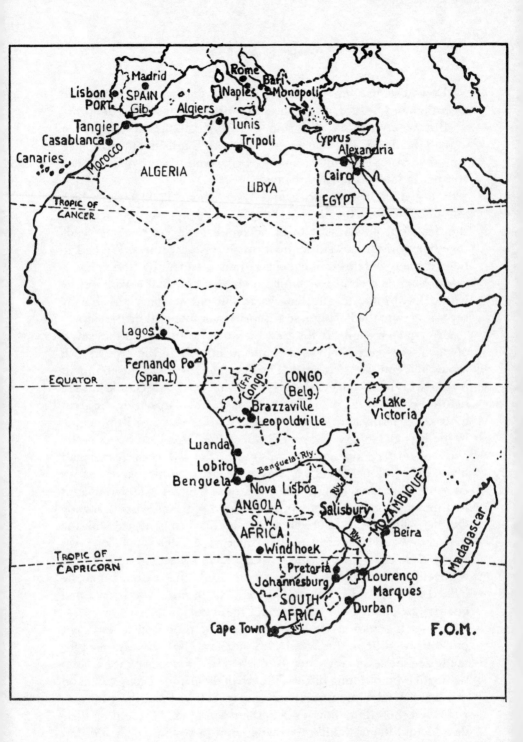

prove necessary.

Captain Briot, in the meantime, was getting anxious about his money. I had sent a message, through Baker Street, saying I needed 40,000 dollars urgently. At first I was instructed not to hand over any money before the ship was surrendered. Then it was agreed I could give him £3,000, with the balance payable once we had taken possession. I knew Briot would not co-operate fully unless he had the total sum first.

As I was not getting very far in my negotiations through Baker Street, the alternative was to go it alone. But where could I lay my hands on 40,000 dollars? My cover as a General Mining representative provided the answer. I went to Luanda and saw a man called Bierman, who was working for an English firm based in Leeds which dealt in mining equipment. Trying to make my story sound as plausible as possible, I told him I needed a short term loan of 40,000 dollars, quickly, to tie up a deal for a shipment of castor beans. His domineering German-born wife, who we believed was an enemy spy, came in while we were talking. She did not say anything as Bierman agreed to lend me the money, interest free, provided I could prove I wanted it for General Mining. I offered him a receipt, which I was not authorised to give. His wife leaned over and whispered to him.

'No, it's not good enough,' he said. 'I will take it only if you can get it stamped officially by the Consul-General, guaranteeing payment.'

That put me in a jam because I was aware the British Consul-General in Luanda, Victor Cusden, could not allow himself to get mixed up in a clandestine mission. Even so, I decided to see him as we had got to know one another well and there was just a chance he might be able to suggest something.

'All I need is the use of your rubber stamp,' I pleaded. 'Absolutely nothing I can do, my dear chap,' he said. 'I would get the sack.'

Then, looking me straight in the eyes, he added. 'I always keep the stamp in the desk. By the way, I must pop out for a cup of tea.' The invitation was obvious. As soon as he had closed the door, I took the stamp and endorsed my phoney receipt.

Bierman was satisfied. He paid me the money in hundred dollar notes. The thought that I was collecting the money from the husband of a German spy appealed to my sense of humour.

I was beginning to think like a criminal, and when Bierman handed me the pack of large denomination notes I had the germ of an idea for making sure the French captain did not just sail away with the cash.

I drove round to the bank and asked them to change the money into small denomination escudo notes, which I put into two large canvas bags. These I took along to my next meeting with Captain Briot. He looked at the bags apprehensively.

'I can't take those,' he complained. 'The harbour police will stop me for sure.'

His reaction was exactly as I had anticipated. I shrugged my shoulders. 'Sorry, it's the best I can do. If I gave you big notes they could be traced.'

In fact I had taken the precaution of arranging with the harbourmaster that Briot should be arrested for attempting illegally to export currency and the two bags should be taken off him if he tried to carry the money aboard his ship. Briot was not in the least suspicious as I had, in his estimation, tried to keep my side of the bargain.

'Could you give me a cheque to be drawn on an American bank?' he asked. I promised to see what I could do. Now at that time the American OSS had in Angola an agent called Vic Violet, a most unlikely name for a six feet six inches tall former New York mounted policeman. Violet, known to his friends as 'the Oil King', was in charge of the Texaco office in Luanda.

I asked Vic if he had an American chequebook. 'Of course,' he said, 'but I haven't got a bean in the account.' He thought it a huge joke when I tore a blank cheque from his book, made it out for 40,000 dollars and signed it with a flourish.

Captain Briot, just like Bierman, was not satisfied with my signature. He also wanted the protection of an official British rubber stamp. The Vice-Consul in Lobito was called Williams, quite a character, a former stevedore in Dakar, and he and I went through the same performance I had enacted with the Consul-General in Luanda. Williams left the room, I used the rubber stamp, and Briot accepted the cheque, which left me clear to return Bierman's money and allay any suspicions his wife might have had.

After the captain had pocketed the cheque, I put the final phase of my scheme into operation. Accompanied by Harbourmaster da Costa, I went aboard the *Gazcon*, pretending to be an interested businessman but really to make sure nothing untoward had occurred and to check if anyone had tampered with the ship's seacocks.

Four or five men from the Portuguese *Policia Internat* – the equivalent of the Gestapo or the KGB – appeared from nowhere and followed us up the gangplank. I felt the hairs rising on the back of my neck. Did they suspect me? The sinister posse kept pace with us all the way through our tour of the ship. I tried not to look in their direction and talked to da Costa about various details of the ship's interior and of my firm's interest in cargoes of seed for conversion into oil.

The International Police were an evil bunch, who would have no compunction about throwing me into one of their vile West African jails if they could prove anything. And what could they prove? It gave me no comfort to reflect that the list of possibilities included espionage, bribery and corruption and conspiring to commit piracy on the high seas, which must have been worth at least ten or twelve years' imprisonment, to say nothing of the disgrace an international incident would cause to me and to Britain.

To my relief our unwelcome escort walked away without saying a word as, back on the quayside, I shook hands with da Costa and bade him goodnight. At least I had satisfied myself there had been no hitch in our arrangements for the *Gazcon*'s departure.

I left the seven newly-recruited and armed Free Frenchmen to deal with the Nazi second-in-command and to handle anyone else on board who showed opposition to our plan.

The next problem was to disguise the fact that the *Gazcon* was getting up steam and was preparing to put to sea without the consent of the Portuguese authorities.

'Tell the harbourmaster you are testing the boilers because they have been inactive for so long,' I instructed Captain Briot. Harbourmaster da Costa was working with us, but I was conscious he would need to have some explanation for his superiors.

It worked like a charm. On three successive days the ship belched smoke as her boilers were 'tested', so that on the evening of the fourth

day it did not look at all suspicious when smoke from her funnel
again drifted across the harbour. This time, however, the *Gazcon*
built up a good head of steam and away she went. A great
commotion swept through the harbour, and there was a half-hearted
attempt to stop her by a Portuguese tugboat, but since the tug's top
speed was eight knots and the *Gazcon* was doing twelve, the chase
was soon abandoned. To divert attention, and to give me an alibi,
I had invited da Costa and other leading figures in the Portuguese
community, to a dinner party at an hotel. I hoped I appeared
completely at ease as I entertained my guests, but my heart was
thumping like a trip-hammer and I tried not to look through the
windows towards the harbour. The party was in full swing when the
Gazcon steamed away. My guests abandoned their food and went
down to the waterfront in response to the commotion, in time to see
the *Gazcon*'s stern disappearing into the evening haze. There was an
uneasy moment or two, during which da Costa and I avoided each
other's eyes, and then the Portuguese decided there was nothing
they could do and we all returned to the hotel, where our festivities
continued until well after midnight.

I had briefed Captain Briot to head for a rendezvous at 9.10 pm
outside territorial waters, having arranged with South Atlantic
Naval Command, Lagos, for the cruiser *Albatross* to be waiting there.

It seems the commander of the *Albatross* decided against boarding
the merchant ship at night-time and waited until morning. The
Gazcon was lost in the darkness, with the result that the two ships
were ploughing about for days, the *Albatross* doing its best to find the
Vichy ship and the *Gazcon*'s skipper trying hard to be found without
making it too obvious. Back in Lobito we had reports of both vessels
being sighted, miles apart, along the coast and I wondered what was
going on.

Through da Costa, an amiable rogue with a criminal record, I
had set up a chain of spies along the coast. 'Da Costa's Mafia' we
called them. These contacts informed me each day of the *Gazcon*'s
position, with the last sighting off Ambrizete shortly before the ship's
final interception. One of the reasons for da Costa's co-operation,
it must be said, was an extra £200 I paid him from my own pocket.
I was comparatively well off during the war, as I had some capital
of my own and I received both a generous salary from General

(*Right*) Bolshevik soldiers.

(*Below*) A victim of the revolution.

(*Left*) Maxim Ganfmann, uncle and newspaper editor, who ate himself to death after release from a Bolshevik prison. (*Right*) Benjamin Manderstam, brother.

(*Left*) Agatha Manderstam, sister. (*Right*) L. H. Manderstam as a young man.

Mining and the pay of a staff major, which was untaxed because even the Inland Revenue was not allowed to pry into the files of SOE. For the most part I did not claim expenses from Whitehall. It could fairly be said that the financial independence of people like myself contributed to the efficiency and success of SOE. In effect, SOE was subsidised by its richer – some might say more criminal – operatives.

Captain Briot, years after the event, claimed the escape and capture spanned nine days but, if memory serves me right, I believe it took the cruiser four or five days to catch the *Gazcon*.

The crew of the *Albatross* shared £50,000 in prize money for taking the *Gazcon*. I received not a penny! As for my phoney cheque, I must give the British authorities top marks – they interned the French skipper but paid him in full after the war.

An aspect which intrigued me was the explanation for his behaviour that Captain Briot would place on record. After all, he could not say he had sold his ship and its cargo for £10,000. For Briot's account of the incident I am indebted to Jean Ebstein-Langevín, a former member of the Resistance, who examined the archives at Vincennes. According to Captain Briot's 'cover up' version, written on schoolpaper, he left Lobito at 20.00 hours on 30 August 1941, after two months of 'laborious negotiations' and after the Portuguese Admiralty had put difficulties in his way, and he was heading for Port-Bouet.

At 21.20, a ship with no lights showing placed itself at the stern of the *Gazcon* and followed her. Briot said he did his best to escape, changing course to the north at 21.50, and then to the east at 02.30. Ten minutes later the ship was lost to sight. But from 16.30 on 2 September to 03.00 on 3 September, the *Gazcon* had to stop while a driving rod was changed. On 7 September the ship was still proceeding slowly because of mechanical trouble. That day, continued Briot, a mast was seen behind the *Gazcon*, belonging to the British cruiser *Albatross*, which at 19.16 gave an order to the *Gazcon* to halt. The order was repeated at 19.23 hours, followed by a warning shot.

At 19.35 the *Gazcon* stopped, after the captain had sent a radio signal and had 'destroyed things', including sabotaging the wheel. At 19.45 hours a boarding party arrived from the *Albatross*, everything was put in order and the ship went to Lagos, where it arrived on 10 September.

That was Briot's story. and it is doubtful if it was believed either by the French archivists or by Briot's employers, the Compagnie de Navigation d'Orbigny. Briot's version did not explain the disappearance of the second-in-command, who was knocked out and thrown overboard. Nor did it say what happened to the ship's log, which followed the Nazi to Davy Jones's locker.

Of course, de Gaulle and the Free French headquarters knew what had happened. But they, like SOE, were not keen to place everything on record. M. Ebstein-Langevin, in a French magazine article about the *Gazcon* 'enigma', pointed out I was known to have been in contact with Colonel Allegret, and so at least one senior French officer had knowledge of the affair. Indeed, I understand our Free French allies were puzzled and annoyed because the ship was not handed over to them. Those members of the crew who did not join the Free French were set free in July 1942.

The *Gazcon* story ended sadly. French records show that the ship was torpedoed, while serving under the British flag, by a Japanese submarine in the Gulf of Aden on 1 September 1942. After the war, I presented a scale model of the *Gazcon* to the Special Forces Club in London.

I was appointed an MBE (Military Division) for the *Gazcon* operation, 'in recognition of gallant and distinguished services in the field'. The recommendation for the award stated I had worked single-handed to:

(a) suborn the captain, 'which required considerable tact and diplomacy';

(b) prevent the scuttling of the ship by the rabid pro-Nazi second-in-command 'which entailed considerable risk in a neutral port under the eyes of an armed guard and the International Police';

(c) pay £10,000 to the captain by borrowing the money 'and by sheer effrontery did so from a businessman who was highly suspect and whose wife was reported to be a German agent.'

The recommendation added: 'throughout the whole of the planning, Major Manderstam exercised great skill, judgment, tact and balance of mind, with the result that the operation was completely successful.'

CHAPTER TEN

Angola Escapades

The Roman Catholic bishop in Luanda was anti-British. He obviously thought the Nazis would win the war and therefore it was prudent for him to support the German cause, an attitude which he made clear whenever we met. I never went to his cathedral and am unaware if he used the pulpit to expound his political views, but his influence was obvious in the columns of the Portuguese language newspaper. Through a mutual friend I had obtained an introduction to the bishop, who was told I was a South African businessman. Such introductions were easy to arrange because life in Angola was so tedious, generally speaking, that anyone of European extraction welcomed a new face and a chance to widen the topics of conversation.

The bishop invited me to his palace at Nova Lisboa, where he gave me an excellent dinner, supervised by his beautiful mulatto housekeeper. They did not realise I understood Portuguese and during the evening they spoke a number of intimate asides to one another in that language. When I was leaving to drive home, I heard the bishop say to her, 'Let's go to bed.' Rumours about the bishop's household were rife in the cocktail, dinner and bridge circles, and there was many a nudge and a wink whenever his name cropped up during the smalltalk.

I discussed with my colleagues, including Captain Niewiarowski – English born despite his name – how best we could nullify the bishop's anti-British stance. Each of us in SOE had been issued with two pills, to be used only in extreme circumstances. One was a suicide L-pill, the other was a knock-out K-pill designed merely to render someone unconscious for several hours. Our scheme involved using a K-pill to compromise the bishop.

Accordingly, we persuaded the Consul-General, Victor Cusden, to act as host at a dinner party, with the bishop as the guest of honour and during which we plied him with a succession of strong drinks. The Consul-General made an excuse and departed with his wife soon after dinner, leaving the bishop, Niewiarowski and myself to carry on drinking. In my case this amounted to swallowing glass after glass of mineral water masquerading as gin and tonics. When he was well oiled I gave the bishop some wine containing the dissolved K-pill. I wondered if he might notice a difference in the taste, but he swallowed the wine without any comment. The drug took about ten minutes to work and then he went out like a light.

We removed most of the bishop's clothes and carefully arranged him on the floor. Then we brought in a black maid, whom I had suitably rewarded, to undress and stretch herself out beside him. I took a photograph of the girl and the bishop in a most unclerical position, after which we dressed him and carried him off to a car and drove him home. His housekeeper thought he had drunk too much, a not unusual occurrence in that household.

Niewiarowski, himself a Roman Catholic, later went to see the bemused bishop. After kissing his ring, Niewiarowski produced a copy of the incriminating photograph, claiming he had found it by accident.

'It's Manderstam,' Niewiarowski explained. 'He is threatening to send the photograph to Rome unless you become pro-British.'

The next issue of the principal local newspaper contained an article in praise of the Allies and although it was not signed, we knew where the inspiration for it had come from. It was in complete contrast to previous articles which had claimed, among other things, that the Nazi bombing raids on British cities were only a retaliation for earlier attacks by the RAF on German towns.

Niewiarowski was involved with me in an operation to test security on the Benguela Railway. The Allies were using the port of Lobito and the railway as a connection with Lake Victoria and the rest of East Africa. On the railway, beyond Nova Lisboa, was a vital bridge, which was a weak link in our supply system. If the Germans blew up that bridge we would be forced to divert all our supplies around the Cape route, which would not only take considerably longer but would also expose our ships to greater danger. Although the Germans used the line themselves, it was realised that their sisal plantations were on the side of the bridge nearest to the port, and sabotage of the bridge would affect them hardly at all.

When the British Consul-General mentioned this to the Portuguese Governor-General he said there was nothing to worry about, his troops were taking good care of the bridge. We were not reassured and so Niewiarowski and I went to check out the arrangements, in the guise of two British tourists.

We found the bridge guarded by a single Portuguese sentry. He looked bored to tears and soon we were chatting in a friendly fashion.

'How do you present arms?' I asked.

He showed me.

'That's quite different from the way they do it in the British Army,' I said. 'Lend me your rifle and I'll demonstrate for you.'

He obliged; I presented arms and Niewiarowski took a picture of L. H. Manderstam pointing a rifle at the unarmed sentry. Our Consul-General was delighted with the photographic evidence to support our request for a tightening of security.

Niewiarowski and I took part in numerous escapades. He was of mixed Russian and Belgian ancestry yet very English in his outlook. His background knowledge of Angola came in useful, as he had worked in Lobito on behalf of an uncle who had shipping and oil interests in the area. I gave Nev a job after the war. He moved on to other employment and some time later I received a telephone call from the landlord of a public house near Piccadilly Circus, saying a customer – a tall man with a black moustache – had collapsed and died of a heart attack on the premises. The only clue to his identity was my visiting card in one of his pockets. It was Nev and he was just forty-five when he died. Pauline, his widow, had been a most capable member of SOE. She became chief buyer in Britain for the Robert Simpson chain of Canadian stores and she married Judge Sir Stephen Chapman (Mr Justice Chapman).

The SOE Mission we established in Angola obtained a bungalow at Luanda, where I stayed with four or five officers serving under my command. Because of my 'cover' it was known as *Il Palazzo de Ricine* (Castor Bean House). We had self-imposed rules. For instance none of the officers was allowed to leave the bungalow after dark, or to go drinking, or to meet people without my permission.

It was a somewhat cloistered existence, full of stresses, not the least of which was the shortage of female company. An officer who had been with us for some time, and who was devoted to his wife, put our nerves on edge each night with his yearnings for the matrimonial bed.

'For Pete's sake, you know where to go,' I said to him. He refused, saying his principles would not allow him to visit a brothel. At first it was a joke, but finally our patience was exhausted and we practically forced him to seek relief. It was quite a performance. He provided himself with all manner of precautions, including French letters, antiseptics and disinfectants. We were almost as tensed up as he was. He came back, much more relaxed and with a huge smile on his face. It did not last long. For three or four weeks he was worrying he might have picked up VD, because in the heat of the moment he had forgotten to use any of his carefuly assembled collection of precautions!

A visit to a brothel by another of our West African operatives caused me a considerable amount of agitation and bother. Our orders were not to let the section's codebooks out of our possession and this man took the instruction literally. When his ship stopped at Madeira and he went searching for sex, he took a codebook with him. He selected a woman and the codebook accompanied them to bed.

The woman must have been good at her chosen profession because she was so successful in taking his mind off the war that he left the book under the pillow when he departed. At least he had the guts to admit it straight away. His confession created a flurry in our dovecotes and we had no choice but to change the code.

One morning a former regular soldier who lived with us at the Luanda bungalow and who had transferred from the Army to SOE, failed to turn up for breakfast and was assumed to have overslept. We thought no more about it until we noticed water seeping under the bathroom door, which was locked from the inside. I dashed into the garden to look through the bathroom window, and I saw the man sitting naked on the toilet and apparently fast asleep while water overflowed from the bath. After breaking the window I climbed in and shook him awake.

'Come on, we're not playing games here. Have you been drinking? Did you leave the house?' I demanded.

'As a matter of fact I did. I had the urge and went to the brothel.'

'Forgiven,' I told him. 'But were you indiscreet; did you let anything drop, other than your trousers?'

He confessed he had been so drunk he had no idea what he had said. This put me in a dilemma. I said I must tell London there had been a serious breach of security and he should be withdrawn immediately. He pleaded with me not to report him. 'The only trade I know is soldiering and this will end my career.' It was unusual for me to let my heart rule my head, but I did not want to destroy a good soldier and let him off with a severe warning.

Some months later, when I was away from Luanda, I received a message saying one of my team, Francis Mills, had died after a mysterious illness. The cause of his death, a few months after his arrival in Angola, was officially recorded as malaria. Mills and Peter Dawson, who had both worked as businessmen in Portugal, had been sent from London to assist in an operation similar to the *Gazcon* affair, and also involving Harbourmaster da Costa. The plan was to capture a German cargo vessel which had taken refuge in Lobito harbour and it was at an advanced stage when the Foreign Office forbade the SOE team to go any further. After the war the German ship was transferred to the Portuguese flag as the *Lugella*.

There were many ways in which we goaded our opposite numbers in the almost unreal situation existing in Angola. One game we had was to put sugar in the petrol tank of the German Consul's car when we found it parked, each time leaving batches of anti-Nazi leaflets for him to read while he waited for a mechanic.

I also used to slip copies of the leaflets into the Consul's letter box during early-morning walks. They were published by the Political Warfare Executive in London and were full of details of Nazi atrocities, not the most pleasant things to read over breakfast.

Portugal did not allow us to have our own radio transmitters and we were forced to use a Marconi clerk to send our signals from Angola to London. In fairness, the same restriction was applied to the Germans. As a result, we made substantial payments to the clerk for the enemy's messages and he collected similar amounts from the Germans for ours. It was a futile, albeit costly, exercise, as neither side could break the other's code.

I was in Luanda one evening, having dinner at an hotel, when my

German counterpart, a Dr Grau, sat down at a nearby table. The opportunity seemed too good to miss so I approached him.

'Good evening, doctor,' I said in German, 'I'm spending a hell of a lot of money buying your signals, which I can't break. You're spending just as much buying my signals, and you can't break them either. Why don't you send me your batch every morning and I'll send you mine? That way we will both make considerable savings for our governments.'

He looked at me with pure hatred in his eyes. 'Impudent Englishman!' he shouted, and he stalked out of the hotel. 'Englander! Englander!' I could hear him rasping as he departed.

Ironically, I was worried that Grau would get his hands on our codes. We had a woman coding officer, the wife of a government official, who was a nymphomaniac and I was afraid she would pass on our codes to any man who slept with her.

I found this out when I was closeted with her in the coding room and she propositioned me. I pointed out her husband was a friend of mine.

'How could I face him after having slept with you?' I asked.

'He wouldn't know,' she said.

I made a point of not getting involved emotionally with any of the women with whom I worked and I made sure the coding officer was quickly replaced. Her weakness was no secret to her husband. When he heard about our fears he took early retirement.

Another 'fun-loving' SOE female employee reported me as a suspicious person when I was attached to our Cape Town office. The man in charge of the office was Richard Broad, formerly of the Seaforth Highlanders, who made an impressive picture in his kilt. When I reported to him he looked at my documents and said they were all in order. 'I'll just signal London about your arrival,' he added, and disappeared into another room. He came back a few minutes later and asked, 'Are you sure your name is Manderstam?'

'Of course. What's all this in aid of?'

'Are you sure your name is not Mr Leopold?'

'Yes. It's Leopold Manderstam.'

'I see. Well, I'm sorry but I can't put you on our strength yet. I must send another signal to London to have a check made on you.'

While this dialogue was going on a secretary came in, an

extremely attractive girl and, from remarks made, it was clear she had alleged I had given a false name. Her face was familiar, but I couldn't place where I had seen her previously.

'What made you say my name was Leopold?' I asked.

She said we had sailed on the same ship, the *Windsor Castle*, from Southampton to Cape Town a couple of years before the war and she had a distinct recollection of my name appearing on the passenger list as Mr Leopold. The penny dropped. As soon as she mentioned the voyage it all fitted into place.

'Now I'm going to tell you something. I have a good memory, too, and I remember you had a terrific bust-up with your boyfriend on the ship and you were picked up with a broken arm in his cabin.'

She blushed to the roots of her hair.

'How did you know?'

'Common knowledge,' I replied. 'The whole blessed ship knew about it.'

Her stormy romance created a minor scandal on the liner. She and her boyfriend were both the worse for drink and she was said to have either fallen out of his bunk or been pushed out.

The confusion over my name was easily explained. I had been entered on the passenger list by my first name only and had not bothered to change the entry.

I could not blame the girl for telling her boss I might be a German spy because I made similar errors myself. Once, when I was flying to Lagos, the DC3 aircraft had engine trouble over the Congo and was forced to land on a primitive airstrip outside Lebango, a notorious centre of yellow fever. The topics of conversation among the local European residents were depressing, being limited to such opening gambits as, 'Poor old Jack died yesterday': or, 'They say Charles has only a few days to go . . .'

I was especially apprehensive as I had failed to have the regulation injections against fever, not through fear of the needle but merely because I thought it was a time-wasting bore. So I used to type out my own medical certificates, saying I had had the stipulated doses and putting faith in my basic philosophy of *che sera sera*.

Sharing a room with me at Lubango's excuse for a hotel was a passenger from the DC3 flight who appeared to be English and who carried himself like a military man.

We regarded one another with intense suspicion because we both had diplomatic bags among our hand luggage and in such circumstance, particularly in West Africa's limited theatre of war, we ought to have known each other. During the time we waited for engine spare parts to arrive we were like Siamese twins, following one another everywhere and each convinced the other was an enemy agent. When I announced my intention to go for a breath of fresh air, he said he would join me; when he proposed a trip to the bar I followed him down. Even when he or I went to the toilet we would come out and find the other nearby, keeping an eye on the door and pretending to be reading a newspaper or a book. After ten days the engine was repaired and our DC3 took off for Lagos, where we were astonished and amused to find ourselves greeted by the same SOE man, who introduced my travelling companion as a British colonel.

CHAPTER ELEVEN

Sabotage

A more sensible person in my position would have played the game by the Whitehall rules and ended the war as a brigadier, or at least a full colonel. But then I would not have been SOE material. As it was, I blotted my copybook time and again, in the opinion of the Foreign Office.

Perhaps the biggest of the wounds I inflicted on Foreign Office susceptibilities was caused by my destruction of the German sisal stores at Lobito. A Nazi called Kuschke owned vast plantations of sisal, used for making ropes, and it was more than I could bear to see loads from his stockpiles being put aboard Portuguese ships at Lobito, en route to Germany for use against the Allies.

During the war some neutral ships operating out of Angola were given so-called Navy Certs, enabling them to go on their way without being searched by the Royal Navy. I did not know, but have learned since, that there had been an unwritten agreement (which would no doubt be denied by the Foreign Office) under which the Germans allowed some British shipments of rubber from Malaya and the Allies let through cargoes of sisal for the German Navy. It was an incredible agreement, and if someone had told me about it when I was in Angola I would certainly not have believed them. The tortuous ways of the politicians and bureaucrats were beyond me. To my mind the problem was a simple one: Kuschke's sisal stores were providing essential supplies to the German war effort and should be destroyed, even though they stood on neutral territory.

I sent an urgent signal to London for permission to deal with the problem. Back came the order, 'You are not, repeat not, to do anything.' On this and similar occasions when I wished to do something against orders I replied, 'Could not decipher signal. Please repeat. Meantime proceeding.'

A violent tropical storm gave me the chance for which I was

waiting. I collected about 3 lb of plastic explosive from a supply I had obtained in Leopoldville and enlisted the help of Captain Niewiarowski. There was no one else about as we drove through the lashing rain to Kuschke's premises. We took our time in planting the explosive and I checked each pencil fuse carefully to make absolutely sure they were in order, for I knew we were unlikely to be given another opportunity. For good measure we threw a couple of gallons of petrol on to the sisal.

The detonation sounded like a tremendous thunderclap and Kuschke's stores were reduced to a smouldering shell. It gave me great pleasure to send a message to London, saying we had just experienced a most awful storm, during which the sisal stores had been destroyed by lightning.

Two signals arrived by return. The first, from the Foreign Office, stated, 'Expect Manderstam's immediate assurance he had nothing to do with it.' I gave the assurance. The second signal made me chuckle with delight. From General Gubbins at SOE headquarters, it contained only two words, 'Well done.'

That was typical of Gubbins, who was never one to be hogtied by conventions. And the same was true of other SOE senior officers. I remember the way Colonel Benham announced my promotion to Acting Major. We were standing alongside one another in the urinals at Hatchett's basement restaurant in Piccadilly when Benham reached his free hand into a trouser pocket and produced a couple of crowns. 'You'd better put these on, Mandy,' he said. 'Congratulations.'

*

When I was not busy with SOE operations in Angola I maintained contacts with the Portuguese and, in my capacity as a businessman, got to know many of the government officials. These included Dr Gusmao, head of the Angola Agriculture Department, who saw much of the SOE team, as part of the 'cover' story was to experiment with the planting of castor seed on behalf of General Mining. My South African trading links also gave me the best possible excuse for spending much time at the British Consulate-General, since Britain looked after South African interests in the colony. In fact we maintained an office at the Consulate-General, on the first floor, ostensibly as a business centre.

It happened that the South Africans wanted to obtain the plans of a landing strip in northern Angola and the man they chose for the mission was a colonel, who had a terrible stammer. He turned up at the Consulate-General, saying he needed to arrange an appointment with the Director of Civil Aviation. He was told he must see me first. With no little effort I managed to interpret each stuttered word.

'Now you be careful,' I said to him. 'The Civil Aviation Director is a very sensitive person. He has to be handled with kid gloves.'

I was aghast when a report of the meeting came back. The colonel had gone straight into the director's office and said, 'I'll give you fi-fi-five hundred p-p-pounds for the p-p-plans of the l-l-landing s-s-strip.'

The director was more than a little perplexed by the entry of the strange South African and felt deeply insulted that a person with whom he had no acquaintance should assume he would accept a barefaced bribe. He ordered the colonel out of the office and telephoned the Portuguese Governor-General. The angry Governor-General then telephoned the British Consul-General, saying, 'If you don't remove that man within twenty-four hours I shall have him arrested.' The colonel was sent home with a flea in his ear, but we were still obliged to do our utmost to get hold of the landing strip plans. They were important because, without the runway specifications and other details, the South Africans could not be sure which of their aircraft would be able to use the airstrip. There was also a suggestion that the Americans might try to use it as a staging post and refuelling station.

I waited long enough for the director to have calmed down and then I went round to see him, adopting my best behaviour. He thought I was English, which gave me an advantage, and I was also experienced in the subtle art of bribing people.

'Your country is our oldest ally,' I pointed out to him. 'I know you sympathise with us.'

'Yes,' he answered. 'I hate the Germans.'

Seizing the opportunity, I said, 'Then will you do a small service for us? We really do need details of the landing strip.'

To my relief he gave a smile and replied, 'With the greatest of pleasure.'

He searched through some papers on his desk, extracted a folder containing the landing strip plans, and handed it to me. I thanked him for his help and said he had been put to a great deal of embarrassment and trouble. As some small compensation he might care to treat his staff to a meal, I suggested, and I should be honoured if he would allow me to foot the bill. I placed on his desk £250, which he accepted without a murmur.

The colonel's visit had one other unpleasant, although fortunately temporary, repercussion. His affliction was so contagious that for several days I found it hard not to stammer.

A little known episode of the war was a scheme put forward by Field Marshal Smuts for the occupation of Mozambique and Angola. He first suggested this in 1941 and I was given the task of smuggling arms for the West African element of the plan, which was codenamed Operation Z. I had a big, two-door Chevrolet, with an enormous boot which had been specially extended up to the front seats, and I used this car to ferry plastic explosive, hand-grenades, ammunition and arms, including machine guns, from Leopoldville to Luanda. The three-day journey covered hundreds of miles of extremely hazardous dirt roads through jungle and dusty scrubland by way of Matadi, Ambrizete and along the coast road.

On one of the return trips I had Louis Franck as a passenger. Although we had strict orders to avoid drawing attention to ourselves and not to commit traffic offences, I was travelling as fast as the pot-holed roads would allow. As we speeded towards a bridge on the approach to Luanda a policeman moved into our path and raised his hand, signalling us to stop. I slowed down and he approached the car. If anyone committed a motoring offence in that part of the world the Portuguese police invariably took the vehicle to a pound, where it was left overnight and examined.

I was in a sweat because of the incriminating contents of the car boot, and I turned to ask Louis what he thought of the situation, only to find myself staring at his back as he dived out of the passenger door and made off down the road. Louis was adept at making himself scarce when there was trouble.

For a moment I was tempted to accelerate, but it would have meant hitting the policemen, who probably knew my car. I decided the best thing I could do was to bluff my way clear. I left the car and began shouting at the policeman in his own language, saying I belonged to the British Consulate and how dare he stop me when I was on important business. I could get him dismissed and may be shot, I yelled. The poor man was so taken aback by this tirade he failed to check whether or not I had diplomatic papers and timidly waved me on. As a matter of fact I did have a British courier's, or diplomatic, passport in addition to my normal South African passport, but it was not to be used unless there was no alternative.

The arsenal we were collecting on behalf of Smuts was hidden in a cellar at the British Consulate-General, unknown to the authorities. As South Africa had no official representative in Luanda, Britain's Consul-General acted for them, which was a convenient arrangement so far as we were concerned, particularly as it ensured the co-operation of the South African Secret Service.

Smuts's Z plan was a closely guarded secret. I have seen no reference to it in literature covering his wartime leadership. But it did exist. Churchill persuaded him to drop the idea, which was just as well, for I'm sure a simultaneous invasion of both Portuguese colonies in East and West Africa, as envisaged by Smuts, would have done little to help the Allies win the war. A few Chevy-loads of arms would hardly have been sufficient for the task, with the result that valuable resources of men and armaments would have had to be diverted from more important areas. There might also have been a propaganda coup for the Germans if the Allies had supported an invasion of neutral territory.

Of course, the South African prime minister and commander-in-chief was putting his own nation's interests to the fore. Long before the war Smuts had expounded his belief that the whole of the East African highlands, from the Union to Abyssinia, could be formed into a white 'European' state, or system of states. And he may have had similar plans for West Africa. He was nearly seventy when World War II started; his memory was going and he was by no means the dominant figure he had been in the Boer War and during World War I. Even in those periods, I believe, his reputation had been built too high.

The projection of Jan Smuts as a war leader, sage and statesman began during the Boer war, when he was over-glamorised for the simple reason that he surrendered to the British. Obviously the British Army commanders wanted to give the appearance they had a very big fish in the net. He was, paradoxically, always more highly regarded in other countries than he was in his homeland, where many saw him as a ruthless, superficial bigot. His nickname was 'Slim Jan,' *slim* in Afrikaans meaning full of guile and deceit. In England, Smuts was treated with the greatest respect and Churchill, in particular, held him in high esteem. During a visit to London in 1942 Smuts attended a War Cabinet meeting and later issued a statement, emphasising the key position that Africa occupied in the 'world struggle'. He stated:

> When Japan entered the war our concern for South Africa and the vital Cape Route was extended to our communications in the Indian Ocean. We did not want a repetition of the Indo-China incident which finally resulted in the loss of Malaya and Singapore and the almost total collapse of the Allied position in the Far East.
>
> Our participation in the East Africa, the Middle East and the Madagascar campaigns has been the result and, considering our slender resources, our contribution has had its value. More and more Africa is emerging as a dominant feature in our war strategy, on which the future of the war will largely depend.

Smuts was influenced by the views of the Dutch Reformed Church, even if he was not such a devout church-goer himself, and South Africa is still paying for his narrow-mindedness. There was a period after World War II when European migrants were queueing up to go to South Africa. I believed as many displaced persons as possible should be allowed in. Even if the first generation turned out to be bad South Africans, I was sure the second would grow up as solid citizens, as happened in America. The ratio between black and white would then be changed.

Smuts was said to lack race consciousness, but he refused to allow unbridled immigration because the Church could not tolerate anyone who was not Dutch Reformed, or at least a Protestant. This

Manderstam (right) with friends in Lourenço Marques before the war.

(*Left*) Major Manderstam in Lagos during his service with SOE's West Africa section.
(*Right*) L. H. Manderstam, centre, in Lourenço Marques during the war, with German Josef
Gerney and a Russian agent.

The Gazcon. The ship's capture, with a valuable car was arranged by Manderst who was awarded the MBE this exploit.

The Chevrolet car which Manderstam adapted to smuggle arms and explosiv Seen outside the Consulate General, Luanda.

The Luanda bungalow whe Manderstam and other age lived. Known as Castor Bea House, because of their 'cc story.

created insurmountable obstacles since most of the would-be migrants were Jews, Greek Orthodox or Roman Catholics. As for the African blacks, the attitude of the Dutch Reformed Church could be summed up as follows: 'God has ordained we should look after the blacks. That is our job. We are the parents, and when a parent punishes a child the child deserves it.'

There was nothing progressive about Smuts. He was far from being my favourite person and yet he was the man to whom I had to report after I had been placed in charge of the West Coast anti-submarine operations.

On my way to see Smuts I went by car from Luanda to Windhoek, in the former German South-West Africa, which had been a mandated territory since 1919 but where the German influence was still strong.

The city was run on German lines; the names of the streets and of the hotels had not been changed, and many of the inhabitants were clearly of German origin. I checked into an hotel, in my uniform, and I asked in German if I could have a bath. My German is good and it obviously fooled the staff, for a few minutes later the hotel owner arrived at my room, smirking and clicking his heels.

'How is it that you, a German, are in British uniform?' he enquired. 'Can I be of any help?'

'PG,' I whispered, meaning I was a member of the Nazi party. 'I am on a special assignment.'

He gasped and whispered back, 'I also am PG.'

We sat down together and, full of his own importance, he told me his story, including the locations of the Nazi cells in the city, and who the principal members were. Of course, I reported all this to the Provost Marshal and the little Nazi and his friends were taken into detention.

After a good night's sleep at Windhoek I flew to Cape Town.

Because of Smut's elevated wartime role, it was decided I should take a jump in rank to 'local' temporary and unpaid colonel for the duration of the trip. Presumably the old man might have considered it an insult if a mere major had been sent to him. And so, dressed in my new finery, I boarded an Air Force plane on a special flight to the military airport outside Pretoria. To my consternation, a guard of honour was drawn up on the tarmac and I was requested about twelve feet tall – and I hesitated at the airplane exit.

When we joined SOE we were taught how to survive, how to kill people with our bare hands, how to blow up factories, but with a shock I realised that I knew nothing about the rudiments of soldiering. I did not even know how to salute properly.

Nothing daunted, I walked with painfully slow and deliberate paces towards the ramrod straight lines of soldiers, trying hard to remember how the King and Monty did it on the Movietone News films. The inspection went without a hitch – at least nobody made any unkind comments in my hearing – and I was taken by car on the final stage of the journey to see Smuts at Pretoria,

A secretary called Miss Richardson received me in an anteroom. She briefed me and added, 'If the old man, when he bids you goodbye, says, "God bless you", you are all right. It means he likes you. If he just says "goodbye", you will know you have not made the grade.' In fact I was with Smuts for about forty minutes, giving details of our plans and telling him how we could fight the U-boat menace around the African coast. At the end of the interview he shook my hand, with the remark 'God bless you'. I had made the grade.

There was a sequel to that meeting, six months later, when I attended a reception at South Africa House, London, in my normal uniform as a major. Smuts was there and he recognised me. He looked me up and down.

'Well, well,' he said. 'Reduced in rank, are you?'

'No, Sir,' I answered, 'I was dressed up solely for your benefit.'

'Serves you right for not being in the South African Army,' he snapped.

I explained how I had tried without success, 'You wouldn't take me.'

'Rubbish,' said Smuts. 'You should have been in the South African Army.'

The trip to London arose from my contention that we should take more positive action against U-boats which refuelled off the West African coast, within supply boat range of Ambrizete, where the Germans kept stocks of diesel oil. We had monitored the comings and going with increasing frustration. Often the enemy submarines came within sight of Luanda and Ambrizete to pick up supplies. In my messages to Baker Street I suggested we should 'doctor' the fuel. I was recalled for discussions and flew to London from Lagos.

Professor D.M. Newitt, the head of our scientific department, listened to my ideas with apparent interest. But he chided me for being impatient. 'My dear chap, this involves research,' he said. 'It will take at least four weeks before I can give you an answer.' He scowled angrily when I took my leave with the remark, 'To blazes with you. I'm not going to wait another four weeks.'

Back to Luanda I went, and I teamed up with Niewiarowski for a raid on the German diesel stores.

I sent Nev to find some latex, which was plentiful in rubber-producing Angola. He had no problem in obtaining four barrels full from a plantation and we transported the latex in a lorry which we borrowed from a coal company. L.H. (Dizzy) Dismore came along to help us handle the barrels, which each weighed about half a hundredweight.

We drove to the diesel store in the dead of night. There were no guards, mainly because the Germans did not wish to emphasise the importance of the place, which was disguised as a Portuguese warehouse, with all the signs and labels written in Portuguese. The store was only two or three hundred yards inland, on the main road, so the drums of oil could be rolled up to the harbour wall.

We worked quickly, opening each of the screwcaps on the oildrums with spanners and then, using wooden trestles to take the weight of the barrels, we poured in liquid rubber with the aid of a metal funnel. The latex mixed freely with the diesel oil, but I knew it would really gum up the submarines' engines. Fortunately, none of the oil drums was filled to the brim before we started our work.

I never knew how many German U-boats were crippled or lost as a result of this operation; how many were stranded on the surface or if any were unable to come up after diving. The repercussions included an increase in police activity and surveillance of all British subjects in Angola, and I heard that irate messages had flown between Berlin, Lisbon and Luanda.

Rosario, the local chief of the *Policia Internat*, made crude attempts to trick me into betraying my involvement. At three o'clock one morning he hammered on my door, waking me up. 'There's a German submarine on the surface, just off the coast,' he called. I was not asleep enough to fall for that. 'It's none of my business,' I shouted back. 'You go to see the Consul-General. Nothing to do with me.'

Another time I invited Rosario to dinner. He kept looking towards the safe where I normally kept a codebook and other SOE material. I had arranged that someone would telephone me during dinner, summoning me to the Consulate-General to receive an urgent message from Johannesburg.

Apologising to Rosario, I hurried away, telling him to carry on without me and having made sure the safe's combination lock was not engaged.

When I returned it was clear he had examined the safe's contents thoroughly, but there was no hint of SOE activities in the papers I had left inside.

All the time I kept up my cover as a General Mining employee while the cat and mouse game with the Portuguese secret police went on. One evening, during a tropical downpour, I looked out of a window and recognised a police agent, who was standing by a lamppost with his coat collar turned up, looking very drenched and miserable. He accepted my invitation to come in out of the rain and I settled him in front of the fire with a glass of whisky.

'By all means snooze off if you want to,' I told him.

So he did, and in the morning I woke him up, gave him breakfast and, despite his embarrassment, insisted on giving him a lift to the police station on my way to the British Consulate-General. Rosario wanted to know how I had twigged the man was on his staff, which I told him was a very silly question in the circumstances.

While I concentrated on Angola, Malcolm Muggeridge, based in Lourenço Marques, was responsible for operations on the east coast. Muggeridge and I were born in the same year and yet we had nothing in common. A Cambridge graduate, a journalist and the son of a Labour MP, Muggeridge was recruited by MI6, 'the proper Secret Service'. Our backgrounds and outlook on life could not have been more diverse. He was, apparently, a sick and depressed man in Lourenço Marques and one of the best known incidents during his service there was a suicide attempt, in which he walked into the sea and then changed his mind.

As Muggeridge was officially employed by the British

Government, on the staff of the Consul-General, his clandestine work was made that much more difficult. Our dealings were mostly confined to the exchange of Nazi signals, and information about U-boat movements in the Atlantic and in the Indian Ocean.

I kept out of Muggeridge's way when I was sent to Lourenço Marques with orders to kill Schwager, the German who was in charge of U-boat operations. Among SOE's 'toys' were many novel ways of killing people and the method of execution we had in mind for Schwager was a very effective poison which gave the victim the symptoms of syphilis. It was intended I should find a way of placing the poison on Schwager's food. Lettuce would have been ideal, because the poison resembled salad oil.

I had mixed feelings about this and I don't know which emotion was the stronger, relief or annoyance, when the Foreign Office vetoed the scheme. Another episode was an operation to capture a stock of industrial diamonds which the German Commercial Attaché in Lourenço Marques was preparing to send to Germany by submarine. General Gubbins, in a signal, told me to organise it and and I immediately sent a reply, 'What about Muggeridge?' To this, Gubbins answered, 'Keep him out of it.'

We happened to know that the Commercial Attaché had an eye for a pretty girl. At the time I had no girls on my staff but an attractive red-haired civilian secretary from our Cape office volunteered for the mission, above and beyond the call of duty. I sent her to Lourenço Marques, where she soon got on to friendly terms with the attaché. One thing led to another and she spent the night with him. She managed to obtain his safe's combination and to remove the diamonds. She was a brave girl.

I recommended her for the MBE, Military Division, but it was rejected on the grounds that she was a civilian and not officially on our strength and therefore did not qualify.

As with Angola, our operations on the east coast had more than a touch of unreality. Among my acquaintances in Lourenço Marques was Josef Gerney, a German who was acting as personal agent for Hermann Goering, and who bought and sold diamonds on the Reichsmarschall's behalf. I'm not sure how he arranged the trade, probably through the skippers of the German submarines prevalent around that coast, and the diamonds more than likely

ended up in Switzerland. The two of us were on good terms with a
Russian called Michalowsky, who was allegedly the Soviet
representative in the Mozambique capital and all three of us were
using the guise of businessmen.

Our agents on the east coast were involved in the Madagascar
campaign, but I did not go there. The Germans had earmarked
Madagascar as a U-boat base early in the war and urged Japan to
occupy the island. A notable success among the SOE activities in
that area was the interception of an enemy convoy off Madagascar,
resulting in heavy German losses. That was due entirely to the three
courageous Mayer brothers, French-speaking Jews from Mauritius,
who took enormous risks. They went on to distinguish themselves
during SOE operations in France.

CHAPTER TWELVE

Economic Warfare

New instructions awaited me when I returned to Angola from the east coast. I was ordered to return to Lisbon and to do so not by my preferred air route but by sea, using a Portuguese ship, the *Musenia*, with a stop in the Azores. Someone in London must have had a real grudge against me, for it would have been difficult to find a more uncomfortable or more dangerous method of transport. My dislike of sea voyages was well known. But much more sinister was the knowledge that Portuguese ships leaving Angola were being stopped by the U-boats and searched for Allied subjects or supplies. If I were captured I could not expect genteel treatment from the Gestapo. All of this would be known to the person responsible for the instruction and I suspected it might be a deliberate attempt to get rid of me.

Shortly before the sailing date, a Portuguese agent called Lemos who supplied information to us and the Germans, buttonholed me.

'Manderstam, I see you're on the passenger list for the *Musenia*,' he said. 'You must be mad. You'll be stopped and taken off. Grau is going to signal to Berlin.

I greeted the news with counterfeit indifference. 'Oh, is he?' I said, and I told Lemos I would give him the equivalent of a hundred pounds if he made sure Grau's message reached Berlin.

'Do you really think the British would let me go on the *Musenia* without a couple of destroyers on hand?' I asked. 'As soon as we are stopped, the Navy will dash in and get the submarine.'

There was not a grain of truth in my statement, but I fooled Lemos and hoped Grau would advise Berlin a trap was being laid. I was, nevertheless, terrified when I went aboard the *Musenia*. My suitcase contained a murderous cache of hand grenades, bottles of petrol and flares, which I intended to use if we were stopped. The danger was greatest after dark, and every night for about two weeks

I slumbered fitfully, listening for any interruption in the beat of the engines. We reached Lisbon without experiencing any sign of U-boat activity. My bluff appeared to have worked.

Once I had settled myself into an hotel and recovered my landlegs I reported to the British Embassy. I had been in Lisbon some months earlier, during a slack period in our Angola operations, when I was instructed to assist the Iberian Section in trying to establish a new organisation for SOE in Portugal and Spain. In the course of that visit I had met David Eccles, later Lord Eccles, who was officially the economic adviser to the British ambassadors in Lisbon and Madrid. He looked at my report and said sternly, 'You have spent three thousand pounds on signals. I'm sorry – I cannot accept this.' After my experiences in Angola I was in no mood for bureaucratic quibbling.

'Three thousand against capturing a prize worth more than four hundred thousand. I risked my neck for Britain and you are haggling over three thousand pounds' worth of cables.'

He shrugged his shoulders. 'You know how it is. They will query it in London.'

'All right, Eccles, if it will make you happy, I'll make you out a cheque now. You can bloody well have the money.'

'Oh, no, I can't allow that.'

'Then shut up,' I said.

He did, and I believe we got on quite well subsequently.

David Eccles ought to have realised that, as we had no transmitter in Angola, we had to pay for all messages sent to London, to say nothing of the hundreds of pounds distributed in bribes to obtain German signals and other information, most of which came from my own pocket.

During my service with the Iberian Section I slipped into Casablanca and Rabat, Morocco, posing as a Dutch civilian, as my Dutch was much better than my French. I sought information about anti-Communist Poles and Russians who were known to be in North Africa and another reason for the trip was to establish useful contacts in preparation for General Mark Clark's Operation Torch invasion, although I knew nothing of the operation plans at the time. We were attempting to check on the strengths and weaknesses of the opposition. General Clark, the US Fifth Army commander, was himself landed in Algeria by submarine to confer with friendly French generals.

On the second trip to Lisbon my mission was 'to report on the leakage of wolfram to Axis countries and to intensify economic sabotage against the Axis.' The supply of wolfram from Portugal and Spain to Germany was a serious problem because of its value to the enemy war effort. It was needed for hollow-charge shells, and tungsten extracted from the ore, with its high melting point, could also be used in alloying steel for armaments and, among other things, for electric filaments. As both the supplying countries were neutral it was difficult to engage in direct action. Top priority was given to making sure any subversive move would not be traced back to me, or to any member of the Iberian Section.

The scheme I evolved in Lisbon, and later used in Spain, was to print forged certificates for the supply of wolfram and to flood the market with them. Speculating businessmen were glad to get their hands on the certificates and did not ask questions about the source. Even the experts could not tell the difference between the forgeries and the genuine issue, a tribute to my left wing friends who arranged the printing. Consequently, hundreds of lorry drivers turned up at the mines, clutching phoney certificates; there was not enough wolfram available to meet the surge in demand and a chaotic situation ensued. The whole process was slowed up and supplies intended for Germany were diverted to the Black Market. After some time squads of police were sent to sort out the tangle of lorries and they stopped some of the vehicles before they reached the mines.

We had a very efficient espionage organisation based in Lisbon, where Sir Ronald Campbell was the British Ambassador. One reason the city was such a hotbed of spies was the amount of shipping which called there on its way to and from the Mediterranean ports, Africa and the Far East. As soon as they disembarked on shore leave, the sailors headed for the red light district, where there was a brothel authorised for the use of British matelots and another for Germans. This was done to reduce the risk of valuable information being passed to the enemy. Our establishment was run by a madam called Magdalena. We had screened the girls, but it would have been naive to suppose none of them was being paid by the Germans to question the sailors about their ships' destinations and their cargoes. After all, we were paying for similar information from girls in the German brothel.

To my chagrin, the German brothel was much better patronised than ours. They offered superior facilities at lower prices and they employed Portuguese touts who watched for British and American sailors and enticed them with the time-honoured words, 'Hi, Joe! I got this lovely senorita for you. My sister. Very clean and cheap.' Ours, by comparison, was a half-hearted venture. The Germans' madam was a sparkling and cultured Portuguese woman, who spoke English and German fluently, as did all the girls. She was charming, but though I spoke to her many times she gave away no information. Her establishment was what the Americans termed 'a real classy joint'.

Most of the shoeshine boys of Lisbon were on my personal payroll, for they saw all the port's comings and goings. As they polished the boots and shoes they took note of any tell-tale insignia on the German uniforms and they listened for a careless word that might give a hint of a destination or the nature of a cargo, all of which details they passed on to me. If a German asked for directions from a shoeshine boy he would make a mental note of it and would tell me later. I was always having to get my shoes cleaned, and whenever I left the Embassy or my hotel I was mobbed by shoeshine boys, yelling, 'Senor! Senor!' and thrusting blackened hands under my nose to accept *escudos* in exchange for mostly useless gossip. But occasionally among the dross were helpful pieces of information.

I was used to operating in neutral countries, where the blackout and bombs were bad dreams, but for me Lisbon was the most attractive city of them all. To appreciate it fully one needed to fly in from London at night time, out of the inky blackness of the Atlantic after a long detour to avoid the attentions of German fighters. Then it came as a shock to see the brightly-lit streets, the well-stocked shops, smartly dressed women and restaurants where rationing was a word never heard.

Lisbon provided many distractions. One evening I met a lovely girl called Almeida at the hotel where I was staying. She accepted my invitation to join me for dinner and we took the entertainment from there. Wiser counsels prevailed next morning and I decided to check with the Military Attaché at the Embassy, to see if there were objections to the way I was spending my leisure hours.

'We know all about her,' I was informed. 'She is a silly little German spy. Carry on, old boy, and if you can get anything out of her, so much the better. But no money should pass between you.'

'What difference does that make?'

'Elementary, old boy. If you can get something out of a German for nothing it's counted as your contribution to the War Effort. But if you pay her, it's trading with the enemy – and that we cannot tolerate!'

The only money I gave to Almeida was the equivalent of £10 to play with in a casino, and she won £130.

While enjoying Almeida's company I was always aware of her ulterior motive in presenting me with her favours and consequently I was on my guard when she tapped on my hotel room door in the early hours of the morning.

'I'm lonely,' she said softly. 'Can I come in?'

'Sorry, I'm much too tired. You go back to your room like a good girl and I'll see you in the morning for breakfast.'

I found out from a member of the hotel staff that Almeida's husband, or at least the man she called her husband, had been standing by, ready to burst in on us as soon as he had given us time to get into bed. He intended to raise Cain in the role of the wronged and outraged spouse and to threaten all kinds of unwelcome publicity, designed to embarrass the British Embassy and to get me sent home.

Ambassadors and I were rarely on the same wavelength. Sir Ronald Campbell did not take kindly to my presence in Lisbon and when I went to Madrid the ambassador there, Sir Samuel Hoare, arranged for me to receive marching orders in less than a week, although I returned to the city several times in the later phases of the war. (The aversion I felt towards the diplomatic class made particularly sweet my part in the liberation of the German Embassy wine cellar, which occurred during one of those later trips after their ambassador had left Madrid. The cellar was renowned for the excellence of its contents and I and a couple of colleagues thought it would be a shame if the ambassador's diligence in amassing such a superb collection of wines should be wasted. We removed the lot and passed the bottles on to people who we knew would appreciate them. As an abstainer, I did not sample any, but the supply was useful to me – access to good wine opens many doors.)

Of course, the political and economic circumstances of Portugal and Spain were very different in the 1940s, exemplified by their capital cities. Lisbon gave the impression of bustling confidence and pro-British sentiment. Madrid was quiet and one could sense the depression of the people. Spain was still recovering from the civil war; food and petrol were in short supply and there was much unrest among the working population. Hoare was intent on placating General Franco, apparently because it was believed he offered Spain the best chance of a stable future. The irony of waging war against one fascist dictator while trying to humour another was lost on Hoare.

The ambassadors deliberately kept a distance between themselves and our work for SOE. We received our orders direct from London, by-passing the embassies, and if anything went wrong the ambassadors could not afford to admit any knowledge of our activities, for fear of causing a diplomatic rift.

In Spain I got up to all kinds of nasty tricks, which was probably a reason for Sir Samuel's dislike of me. But I could console myself with the knowledge that Franco did not like *him*. One person who did get on well with Franco was Thomson of the Treasury who, while attached to the Madrid Embassy, had been instructed to keep an eye on me. He was one of the few Englishmen who had direct access to the Spanish leader, partly I suspected because Franco was impressed by Thomson's conversion to Roman Catholicism. Rather than being a stooge for Hoare, Thomson became my friend and he poured oil on a number of patches of troubled water I left in my wake.

To an outsider, or establishment figure, many of SOE's actions might have appeared frivolous and not cricket. Yet they all had a deadly serious purpose, to upset the enemy and to delay or disrupt the German war machine in any way we could.

A particularly hilarious wheeze I perpetrated was the introduction of itching powder into German Army uniforms. I had become friendly with a pro-British Spaniard called Perez, who was employed by a textile firm which supplied cloth for German uniforms. We were spending an evening together when Perez told me he would give a king's ransom to hurt Franco or the Nazis. Perez worked in the textile plant's finishing department where the cloth was rolled up, ready for transportation, which was the ideal place to interfere with the shipments. I sent to London for two kilos of finely milled glass, so fine it would penetrate the skin without cutting, thus causing a severe itch and possibly a nasty rash.

I never ceased to be amazed at the way our SOE backroom boys and girls could lay their hands on anything at short notice in wartime. The bags of powdered glass arrived from London, through the usual channels and the stock came not from SOE stores, I was told, but from a joke shop. If that were so, the joke shop owner must have thought it was his lucky day, for it was probably his whole supply.

Perez smuggled the itching powder into the factory and sprinkled it on to batches of cloth as they went through the final rollers. We laughed fit to burst at the thought of German soldiers scratching themselves to death as they went into battle.

On a flight to Lisbon I had first hand experience to support my conviction that Irish people are much more wily and mentally nimble than their music hall image would have us believe. I was a passenger in a Sunderland flying boat which developed engine trouble over the neutral Irish Republic and we were forced to put down. All the passengers and crew were British officers, including a very Blimpish brigadier, although we were in civilian clothes. An Irish Customs officer examined our baggage and, as luck would have it, the first case he opened was Blimp's and there, right on top of the clothes, was his brigadier's tunic. The Irishman looked at the uniform, with its red tabs, medal ribbons and insignia and he said, evenly and with commendable presence of mind, 'This is an air warden's uniform, isn't it?'

Our brigadier flushed with hurt pride and indignation and like a damned fool blurted out, 'Of course not, man. Surely you can recognise a British officer's uniform?'

Goodness knows what the consequences might have been, as we were all on active service. Visions of internment passed before our eyes, but the Customs man was equal to the situation. He looked steadily at the brigadier.

'No, sir. I'm sure you are wrong. It's an air warden's uniform.'

A dig in the ribs from another officer ensured the brigadier got the message this time. No further questions were asked, the engine was repaired and we went on our way after a stay of nine days in the republic.

CHAPTER THIRTEEN

Around the Mediterranean

In 1943 we received reports of Russians in Italy, some of them serving with the Axis forces, and I was instructed to try to infiltrate a Soviet agent, in the hope that he could make contact and organise subversive activity. The Royal Navy went to great lengths to place a submarine at my disposal and we picked up the agent at Algiers. He was white as a sheet when he clambered aboard, but I did not regard his pallor as significant since all landlubbers were apprehensive about travelling in submarines.

We nosed into the Mediterranean and dived and I noticed that the further we went the more agitated our Russian friend became. At last we surfaced in pitch darkness off Naples, where the Russian adamantly refused to be landed. I spent some time trying to persuade him but he would not be budged. Finally the skipper, in terse Naval fashion, said he could hang about no longer and we returned to Algiers. Admiral Cunningham, commander of the naval element of the Torch force, was extremely annoyed when he heard about the Russian's attack of funk. The admiral had loaned us a sorely-needed submarine just to land one man.

One of my superior officers defended me, asking, "What else could he have done?"

'He should have thrown the bastard overboard and come back and reported, "Mission accomplished",' said the admiral. The hapless agent was delivered back to his comrades and we heard no more of him.

I was attached to an SOE outfit in Algiers which used the cover name 5th Special Signals. The port was a stepping-stone to Italy. Later on, after the invasion of Italy, I was shipped to Naples and again my brief included liaising with the Russians who were serving on our side, and watching out for information about the White Russians who had settled in the country or who were serving with the Italians or Germans.

There was little for me to do in Naples and I was sent across Italy to the port of Bari, on the Adriatic coast, where No 1 Special Force operated, under Commander Gerard Holdsworth. I obtained a place aboard a DC3 aircraft, which seemed the quickest and safest method of transport. Unfortunately, it was a really filthy winter's day when we flew over the Appenines.

As we tried to get above the weather and approached the DC3's ceiling of around 18,000 feet, the pilot announced, 'Sorry, chums. I've got sufficient oxygen for the crew, but not enough for you lot. You will pass out, but don't worry, once we lose height you'll come round.' Charming, I thought. I became very dizzy and perishing cold but I, and one other passenger, managed to stay conscious.

While I was in the Bari area there occurred one of the most devastating incidents of the war, which was hushed up until well after hostilities ceased. An American vessel, the *John Harvey*, carrying a top secret cargo of a hundred tons of mustard gas – the sort used in the trenches during the First World War with such hideous effect – was bombed by the Luftwaffe. The town received no warning about the lethal nature of the cargo and consequently no one foresaw the danger from the poisonous cloud drifting across the harbour, caused by the liquified mustard gas mixing with the oil on the water.

My flat was on the sixth floor of a block some distance inland. From the window I could see the ships unloading, with their lights on and no attempt at blackout, because it was thought a German bomber attack was only a remote possibility. The first I knew of the raid was the 'crump' of bombs and the sound of ammunition blowing up.

More than two thousand civilians and military personnel were killed by the gas and by the bombs which destroyed seventeen ships and badly damaged eight others. We, in SOE, were as much in the dark as the townspeople and, like them, treated it as a straightforward air raid. Fortunately, none of our men came in contact with the mustard gas.

A casino had been set up in an officers' mess at Bari, where British, American, French and Russian soldiers could take their ease and enjoy a beer or two. One afternoon I walked into the casino and saw a Russian colonel trying, without success, to explain to an

(*Left*) The 'cloak and dagger gang', in Luanda. Group includes, back row *r to l*, OSS agent Vic Violet, Manderstam, vice-consul Bringis. Niewiarowski is immediately in front of Manderstam and sitting in front is Hedley Vincent. (*Right*) The Italian ship Duchessa D'Aosta, in Lagos harbour after its capture.

Louis Franck, head of SOE's West Africa section – centre, front row – watching a wartime football match in Lagos.

(*Left*) Brigadier Colin Gubbins receiving a Polish paratroop badge from General Sikorski, 1941. (*Right*) Field Marshal Smuts.

(*Left*) Mr Harold Macmillan with General Alexander, North Africa, 12 June 1943. (*Right*) General (later Field Marshal Sir Gerald) Templer.

English batman, in Russian, that he wanted a drink. I approached and asked, also in Russian, 'Can I be of any help, colonel?' He started like a shot rabbit and hurried away without another word. The man apparently reported our encounter, because the head of the Russian Military Mission in Bari, who was not a fervent Communist, warned General Gubbins that an NKVD man was dressed as a British officer. Gubbins, on a visit to Italy, thought it a huge joke. At the earliest opportunity he took me over to the Russian and said, 'Here is your NKVD man. He is one of my best officers.'

Among the SOE officers at Bari was Captain A. R. (Dick) Cooper, a remarkable man, who had won the Croix de Guerre at the age of sixteen while serving in Gallipoli with the French Foreign Legion in the First World War and who spent more than eleven years in that toughest of fighting units. Dick could speak all of the Mediterranean languages like a native and hypnotism was among his many skills. I was a sceptic, but I was converted when I saw him put some of our colleagues 'under the influence'. There was no trickery about it, yet when he tried to hypnotise me he failed. We both had strong wills and I could not relax sufficiently to allow another person dominate my mind.

I did not stay long in Bari before making a short journey down the coast to Monopoli, where an SOE group was working with Italian partisans on a plan to infiltrate guerilla fighters into Rome ahead of the Allied troops. Most of our efforts in that area were focussed on the Army's drive towards Rome, which had been halted at Monte Casino. A friend of mine, Hedley Vincent – who had taken over from me in Angola – was working on the infiltration. Vincent was later flown across the Adriatic and parachuted into Jugoslavia. He walked from there across the border into Northern Italy, where he organised partisan groups and he was able to send back information to me about the Cossacks who had hoped to take up the Germans' promise of a 'new homeland' for them in the Fruili-Venetia Giulia region, on the edge of the Carnic Alps. Hedley's work in Italy was recognised with the award to him of the DSO.

Part of my job in Italy was to help arrange the local supplies of food, ammunition, rifles and other equipment being air-lifted to the Jugoslav partisans. The stores which were under my jurisdiction also included cases of wine for the officers' mess. One of these cases, of a particularly fine wine, went missing and not until long after the war did I find out what happened to it. I was in Switzerland to have a hip operation at a Berne clinic, where a doctor on the staff turned out to be a former Jugoslav partisan. We had many a chat about the old times, during which we discovered he had been on the receiving end of the supply drops I had organised.

A funny thing happened, he said. They had been expecting a supply of ammunition, but among the containers dropped by parachute from our aircraft was a case of good wine, which landed undamaged and which they had enjoyed enormously. It could not have gone to a better cause.

I was anxious to do more during my time in Italy. I should have liked to have gone over to Jugoslavia, but I was not asked. Perhaps I was regarded as too adventurous. My superiors no doubt did not trust me to co-operate fully with others in the field, as I was so bad at taking orders. I recall General Gubbins asking me to dinner after he had succeeded Hambro as SOE's executive director and introducing me with the words, 'This is Manderstam, my biggest headache. It is all I can do to prevent him becoming a hero.' Gubbins accepted me as I was, warts and all, and for that reason we remained on most amicable terms.

I spent Christmas 1943 in Cairo, attached to the 133rd Special Force. Among my tasks was the interrogation of men serving with General Anders's Polish Corps, many of whom were claimed by the Russians as Soviet citizens. Some had left their homeland shortly before Germany invaded and thus had information of value to us.

As usual I set off with every intention of ensuring my stay in the Middle East was as comfortable as possible. But I received a nasty shock when I arrived, late at night, by air. I was told to go to the Officers' Transit Camp, which turned out to be a terrible place. It was filthy. The linen was foul and the whole camp stank.

Late as it was, I resolved not to sleep there. I carried my belongings to the camp commandant's office, where he was still burning the midnight oil, and informed him I was going to get a room at Shepheard's Hotel, the best in Egypt. He smiled a knowing smile, as if he had heard that story many times. There was absolutely no chance of a mere major getting a room at Shepheard's, he said, it was very late and, in any event, the hotel was permanently full of top brass and other VIPs. Perhaps the commandant had not travelled widely. He was looking at the crowns on my shoulders, whereas I was thinking of the thick roll of banknotes in my pocket.

At two o'clock in the morning I arrived at Shepheard's, travel weary, thirsty and dying for a nice soothing bath. The clerk who was manning the reception desk looked up with an obvious lack of interest, casually observing my crumpled appearance and the case I carried.

'We do not have any rooms available, sir.'

I dumped my case alongside his desk, removed my cap and reached for the hotel register.

'I'm sorry, sir, we do not have any rooms available,' he droned, like a gramophone with its needle stuck.

His eyes widened as I produced the bankroll and counted pound notes, one after the other, beneath his nose. When I reached ten, he roused himself from his torpid state to say, 'I think I may be able to fix you up with another officer, if you double up.'

'No,' I said firmly, 'I'd like a room of my own,' and I went on counting. At fifteen I stopped and looked at him and he said, 'I believe I can find a single room, but without a bath.'

Not good enough, I told him. I resumed the count. I got to twenty before he reached out a hand with the remark, 'Sir, I've just remembered. I have a room with a bath for you.'

Next day, refreshed after a bath and a good night's sleep, I reported to the 133rd Special Force, commanded by General Stawell, whose adjutant introduced himself and apologised for the dismal, uncomfortable quarters which had been allocated to me.

'But I'm perfectly all right,' I told him. 'I'm staying at Shepheard's.'

He stared in disbelief. 'I couldn't even get the general in there. How did you do it?' I explained my simple technique and offered to do the same for the general, an offer he accepted.

*

I was in Egypt for two or three months, for the most part kicking my heels in Cairo and Alexandria. The native districts, where all the fun happened to be, were out of bounds, for reasons of security and for our personal safety as there was always the danger that an unwary soldier would be found down an alley with a knife in his back. We were not supposed to be seen in nightclubs, nor were we allowed to frequent other places of entertainment. But we were not inhibited by the rules. On New Year's Eve, for example, we made up a party with a few Wrens, in civilian clothes, and disappeared for the night.

On a previous visit to Cairo I had met 'Wild' Bill Donovan, head of the Office of Strategic Services, the American equivalent of SOE. I was supposed to pay my respects and to discuss with him one or two operations which were being planned. Donovan was a brilliant but impossible man, who enjoyed the confidence of President Roosevelt and who was used to getting his own way. A bone of contention we discussed was the demarcation line between SOE and OSS, which gave rise to heated exchanges. I was aggressive and outspoken when I was younger, a trait that did not endear me to some senior officers, and I told Donovan the OSS had no right to claim credit for SOE achievements, especially as SOE was responsible for his organisation coming into existence.

'You remind me of a bunch of bananas,' I added, 'some green, some yellow and some just rotten.'

The remark angered him and he snapped back, 'You're not only addressing a general of the US Army, you're also addressing a Philadelphia lawyer. I'll get even with you.'

When I left him I asked his adjutant what Donovan meant by calling himself a Philadelphia lawyer. 'He meant a shyster,' said the adjutant.

My antipathy towards the OSS went back to my days in Morocco, when Donovan's men had taken over the work I had started and they grabbed all the credit.

The OSS were not miracles of efficiency. If we had been given the facilities they enjoyed we would have been able to achieve much more. They received greater financial backing, they had the best equipment and they had more personnel. In the early days all the OSS men were trained in Britain and I used to tell them, 'There is one area in which you will never beat the English – they are six hours ahead of you and always will be.'

I spent three weeks with an OSS unit in Rabat, trying to get to know their ways, and I was staggered by their indiscipline. God knows we in SOE were not slaves to the military manuals, but we were paragons compared with them. It made my hair curl to see a sergeant sitting on the edge of his commanding officer's desk and addressing the colonel by his first name. But one compensation at the OSS unit was the food, which was wonderful. The Americans served up for us five-course meals, including ice cream, which were very much better than the wartime fare at Buckingham Palace.

CHAPTER FOURTEEN

The Russian Section

Early in 1944 I was appointed head of SOE's Russian Section. By that time planning for the invasion of Europe was well under way and we felt victory could not be long delayed.

Among the effects on me had been a recall to England to take part in an SOE refresher course for field officers, at Liss, in Hampshire. The CO was an Irish Guards officer called Grayson, one of the old school and he took an instant dislike to me. His attitude was made clear soon after we met, when he told me, in the tone of a headmaster talking to a thirdformer, 'There are three things which one does not discuss in the mess – one's regiment, politics and women.'

'Then what the hell do you talk about?' I said.

'Well, there's sport; there's such a thing as cricket, there's rugby, there's boxing, there's tennis . . .'

I was completely lost for a reply, although several good rejoinders occurred to me later.

The highlight of the course was a seventeen-mile forced march in full kit, which I had to complete in four-and-a-half hours during the night, leading seven men to a rendezvous. I saw no future in that kind of exercise, so I went into Liss and hired two taxis. We reached the rendezvous within the hour and thus had plenty of time to make tea, to eat our rations and have a snooze before the CO arrived.

'Well done, men!' he exclaimed. 'How on earth did you get here in such good time?'

His face was a picture when I replied, 'Very simple, sir. You told us to use any means available, so we took a couple of taxis.'

A heavy guard had been put around the house and grounds where we were staying and Grayson ordered us to go out and to infiltrate our way back without being challenged. All I did was to find a convenient thick bush in the grounds and sit under it for a couple of hours before strolling into the house. The others went well away from the area and, on their return, not one managed to get past the sentries. Grayson had to give me top marks because I did not confess I had failed to play the game by the rules.

Another exercise we were set by the CO underlined the difference between my way of thinking and the average English officer's approach. We were told a very important document was kept at an imaginary place in central France, guarded by six SS men. The objective was to get the document. All sorts of suggestions were put forward, the mildest of which involved the dropping of fifty paratroopers.

I asked the man in charge of the exercise, 'Do the Germans have regular sentry duties?'

'No. They stay in the room with the document.'

'Do they drink coffee?' I went on.

'Oh, yes, certainly every morning.'

'Who delivers the milk?'

'A local peasant, most probably.'

'Have we got a Maquis there?'

'One must presume we have.'

'Then,' I said, 'why don't we poison the milk and send one man in to cut the telephone and retrieve the document?'

As a result of that exchange, Grayson sent for me and said, 'One can see you are a foreigner. No British officer would suggest a thing like that.'

I told him the lives of fifty paratroopers were more important than the principle of not poisoning an enemy.

Grayson, in his report to General Gubbins, gave me good marks for being reasonably intelligent and for being well read. His conclusion: This man is not fit to be a staff officer.

When Gubbins showed me the report, I commented, 'Well, sir, this looks like it!'

'Not at all,' he replied. 'In fact you can be my personal staff officer.'

*

My work for the Russian Section took me back to Italy, where the airlift of supplies to the partisans in Jugoslavia and to the rest of the

Balkans was being increased. It was a routine fact-finding trip, during which I met a number of Soviet officers for talks and again sought information about the Russian exiles. But there was nothing routine about the first leg of my journey back to England, by way of Cyprus and Cairo.

I was foolish enough to hitch a lift in a US Air Force Liberator bomber, which was flying from Bari to Cyprus. My misgivings began as soon as I climbed aboard and caught the whiff of bourbon on the American pilot's breath as he half rose to greet me. I realised he was drunk, or at least heavily under the influence. The aircraft was fitted with extra fuel tanks inside the fuselage and I had to sit on the floor in between the tanks. I complained of an icy draught, and the pilot swung round in his seat with a malevolent grin. Shouting to make himself heard above the noise of the engines, he informed me he had only to press a button and I would be in a much bigger draught because I was sitting on the bomb bay doors. The fuselage was so cramped I was forced to huddle there for the whole flight, shivering not only from the cold but also at the thought of how one nudge from the drunken pilot would jettison me into the sea. I am not a religious person, but I breathed a silent prayer of thanks when we eventually bumped down in Cyprus. Several days in Cairo, which was the SOE base for the Balkans, helped me to recuperate.

Soon after my return to London, I was told to report to Southampton on D-Day plus three, with orders to join No 3 Special Force attached to 21 Army Group. The Transport Officer at Southampton informed me that, as I was the senior ranking officer on the vessel taking me across the Channel, I would be 'OC troops' for the voyage. These Army abbreviations confused me. I knew a CO was a Commanding Officer. But the term OC meant nothing to me and I had no idea what I was supposed to do. My ignorance must have shown, for an Irish Guards sergeant, who was standing listening with interest to the conversation, came to my rescue.

'Don't worry about a thing, sir,' he said reassuringly. 'Tomorrow morning, half past six, kit inspection before we go. I'll be there to make sure the men are ready. I'll come to you and say, "All present and correct, sir!" and you just say, "Carry on, sergeant!" Nothing to it, sir.'

It all went like clockwork, just as he had promised. Simply for effect I walked along the lines of soldiers and prodded a few items of equipment, nodding as I did so. The sergeant took over and saw the men were all embarked safely on the landing craft which took us to France. When it was over I slipped the sergeant a £5 note to express my gratitude.

We went ashore near Arromanches, on what had been designated Gold Beach for the invasion. The Mulberry Harbour, which had been towed across the Channel, was still in place and the wreckage of battle was everywhere. No 3 Special Force had already established a base, under canvas, and I joined my colleagues there. We each had our tasks to do and my own priorities were to contact Resistance leaders and to find ways of persuading as many as possible of the Russians who were serving with the German forces to lay down their arms.

The Maquis members whom I interviewed in France were basically of two types. The Communists were by far the most brave, effective and professional. Most of the others were panic-stricken and not nearly as courageous as they later tried to make out; many of them were looking for political insurance which they thought would come in handy after the war. Here I am speaking only of my personal experience.

The Communists were of particular help to me in obtaining details of Russians who were serving with the Germans. Despite their political convictions, the Communist Maquis did not believe we should repatriate any Russian prisoners against their will.

There were thousands of Russians wearing German uniforms in France and they were in the most unenviable predicament. Almost without exception they had enlisted in the German Army to fight Communism in their homeland, to escape summary execution, or to avoid starvation. The last thing they wanted was to fight the British and the Americans. A large number of them had joined the Russian Liberation Army formed by General Andrei Vlasov, the former Soviet officer who was captured in 1942 and who, somewhat naively, decided he could combat Bolshevism by fighting alongside the Germans.

Following orders, I toured the forward positions and, using a loudhailer, delivered a message in Russian to the opposing troops, rather as the Chinese broadcast from the hilltops during the Korean

War. I asked the Russians to surrender, saying I knew they did not wish to fight us; that they would be given assistance to travel to America, or any part of the British Empire, and they would be allowed to assume new identities.

The message carried conviction because I believed the Allies would honour these promises, and it was backed up by leaflets which assured the Russians they would be treated fairly, according to the Geneva Convention.

Partly through these efforts, thousands of Russians surrendered and came over to our lines, forming a large proportion of the 14,000 troops who were soon ensconced in a prisoner of war camp. I interviewed dozens of the Russians and, when batches of prisoners were transported to England, I followed them to continue the questioning at camps in Surrey and Yorkshire.

In my investigation of the White Russians' role in the war I also interviewed German officers, some of them at the London District Cage, the Interrogation centre set up in a 'Millionaires' Row' mansion in Kensington Palace Gardens, under the direction of Lt-Colonel A. P. Scotland. Colonel Scotland had gained invaluable knowledge of the Germans while serving with their Army in South-West Africa forty years earlier. From some of the German officers I obtained statements which supported the stories I had heard of how many of the Russians had been forced to serve the Nazis.

*

The long arm of coincidence has reached so often into my life that I'm rarely surprised by the most unlikely of encounters. When I was involved in the interrogation of prisoners I was sent to Leeds to question an SS medical officer. He was said to be an awkward customer, who refused to give any information about himself. A soldier brought the man to a room I occupied in a requisitioned house. Trying to put him at ease, I greeted the prisoner in German and offered him a cigarette.

'I am not taking anything from a damned British officer,' he snarled as he drew himself stiffly to attention.

I placed some sandwiches in front of him because I knew he was on a meagre diet. He shoved the plate back across the desk.

Determined not to allow the man to annoy me, I smiled and asked if there was anything else he wanted. Until then he had been staring at the wall several inches above my head, and for the first time he looked directly at me.

'Your face is familiar,' he said, hesitantly. 'Is your name Manderstam?'

'Look here, my dear chap,' I answered, 'I'm asking the questions. You are not interrogating me.'

From his dramatically changed attitude, however, I could see there was more in it than the casual dropping of a name.

He persisted, 'Did you have a sister, Agatha?'

'Yes, that's right,' I confirmed, slightly put off guard by the mention of Agatha's name.

'Well, my name is May. I was her fiancé when we were in Jena.'

He gave a deep sigh, sat down in the chair I had offered to him, and he told me his full story.

Against my advice, Agatha had stayed in Jena at the outbreak of the war and, after Hitler's Operation Barbarossa had overrun the Baltic States, she had gone to our home town, Riga, where she believed her training as a doctor would be of greater use. I knew she had a boyfriend in Jena, but I had never met him.

Agatha was very German-orientated and obviously felt she was safe when she went to Riga. But the Gestapo arrested her during the purge of the Jews, solely because her surname sounded Jewish. There was no trial, no attempt to check her background; they did not even give her a chance to explain. They just took her away and shot her.

It was a chance-in-a-million I had come across her German fiancé in a prison camp in Leeds, and an even longer shot that he had recognised me simply from the family likeness Agatha and I shared.

*

I went back and forth across the Channel several times after D-Day. Most of the time, while we were in France, the No 3 Special Force slept in tents. One of these encampments comprised the most luxurious tented accommodation I had ever experienced. Each tent had a bath with running water, and I even had a batman. But by the time we reached Paris I was disenchanted with tents, especially as the one allocated to me at a camp in the Chantilly area had seen better days, and there was not a bath in sight.

I reported to my old friend L. H. Dismore, who had joined SOE's RF Section, which worked in co-operation with de Gaulle's headquarters.

'What about a hotel?' I asked Dismore, who knew Paris well, since he had worked there as a *Daily Mail* journalist.

'They are full of Yanks,' he said.

He agreed to lend me a jeep, so I could drive into Paris, and he called after me as I left, 'You'll never get a hotel room, Mandy. There's a war on, you know.'

The French capital was in a chaotic state, but eventually I found an American billeting officer. Army personnel in Europe were issued with forms called Chef's Movement Orders, which had to be date-stamped alongside the name of the outfit to which you were attached. I had a Movement Order, which Dizzy had failed to complete. I am not sure whether his omission was by accident or design but it was fortunate for me, because if it had contained the name of the unit at Chantilly, the Billeting Officer would have directed me back to the tents. As it was, he asked for the Movement Order and remarked, 'Well, it's dated, but where were you yesterday? What outfit are you with?'

I looked him straight in the eye and, grinning like a schoolboy, said, 'Please, Captain, don't ask silly questions. I came straight here and you know where one spends the first night in Paris.'

He smiled back. 'Fully understand,' he said, and he gave me a room at the Crillon, one of the best billets in Paris, where we had American rations and French cooks. Poor Dizzy was flabbergasted when I invited him to join me for a meal at the Crillon.

'How the bloody hell did you manage to get in here?' he wanted to know.

'Just a little bit of initiative and enterprise,' I answered modestly.

On one of my trips back from France I bumped into the film actor David Niven at Cherbourg. He was wearing the uniform of a full colonel and I was going through another of my metamorphoses as a lieutenant-colonel, local, unpaid. We were both in a hurry to get back to England and in my case I had a top priority order to return

as quickly as possible to London. The only vessel heading in that
direction was a motor torpedo boat, bound for Harwich, with room
for just a single passenger. The officer who was in charge of transport
looked at our papers and said to me, 'You've got Operational Orders
– climb aboard.'

Niven was terribly cross and tried to pull rank. 'How dare you,'
he shouted at the man. 'I'm a colonel – he's only a lieutenant-
colonel.' The tone of his voice and the look of scorn on his face also
implied that, from my accent and manner, he had discerned I was
not even an Englishman.

Wartime Transport Officers were a tough bunch, and this one
was not a man to be brow-beaten. I got the place, but in a very short
time I wished I hadn't been so keen. A young second lieutenant had
offered me a tot of rum just before we left harbour and, when I told
him I didn't drink, he said, 'Are you sure you won't make an
exception? It's a bit rough out there.'

We had barely cleared the harbour before I realised what he
meant. For about three hours the MTB bucked and skipped at up
to 50 knots, like a beer barrel hurtling through rock-strewn rapids,
and I was sick as a pig.

Some years later, my wife and I were having dinner at a
restaurant in Antibes when we noticed David Niven with his wife
and two children at a table nearby.

'I wonder if I should approach him?' I asked my wife. 'Do you
think he'll remember me?'

'For God's sake, no,' she advised. 'He's very aggressive and can
be most unpleasant.'

I took her advice, but I was sorely tempted to tell him how much
I regretted pipping him to the post and making that MTB trip.

*

Among the agents I helped to brief before they went on missions
behind enemy lines was Wing Commander 'Tommy' Yeo-Thomas,
whose adventures were recounted in Bruce Marshall's book, *The
White Rabbit*. The part of Tommy's briefing left to me was to impress
on him the importance of trying to discover where the Russian 'exile'
divisions had been sent and to find out their attitude to the German

Army. My last words to him before he departed were, 'Bring back
a bottle of perfume from Paris.'

That was for Tommy's second mission into France, during which
he hoped to rescue his friend, Pierre Brossolette. As it turned out,
Brossolette died in attempting to escape from the Germans in Paris
and Yeo-Thomas was himself captured, tortured and thrown into
the notorious Buchenwald concentration camp. Tommy escaped in
dramatic circumstances. By chance, I happened to be with the 21
Army Group when he turned up and, having briefed him on the way
out, I debriefed him on the way back. Some of the details I recall
him giving to me differ from those recorded in *The White Rabbit*.

Tommy was a marvellous, brave man (he was awarded the GC
and the MC). With a mixture of French and Welsh blood in his veins
he was, however, a womaniser. One of the first things he did when
he returned to France was to contact a French girlfriend and arrange
to meet her at a Paris Metro station. The girl, in the meantime, had
acquired a Gestapo boyfriend and she betrayed Tommy. The
Germans really made a mess of him. They beat him, they poured
petrol over his groin and set it on fire, they put him in a bath full
of water and ice, but they could not break Tommy.

As I recall, he told me he had informed a German doctor that,
if the doctor would assist an escape, Tommy would put in a good
word with the Allies to save the doctor from execution for war
crimes. The invasion Army was well into Europe and the Nazi
officers were beginning to look for ways by which they could save
their skins. Tommy had earlier prolonged his own life by exchanging
prison clothes with a dead Frenchman, knowing that the meticulous
guards would check the number on the corpse's uniform and would
assume Tommy had died.

The German doctor said he would like to help, but the only way
he could think of was to give Tommy an injection of morphine, in
the hope that he would be thrown outside the camp with the corpses
awaiting cremation. He might be taken for cremation on the same
night. But, if lucky, it would be the next day, which would give him
the chance to recover consciousness and to run away.

Tommy told me he came round during the night, cold as ice, and
he found himself buried under six or seven bodies. He wriggled out
and made off. Eventually, he managed to find his way across the

Allied lines to freedom. He was emotionally disturbed and in an awful physical state after his harrowing experience.

While he was with the 3rd Special Force, attached to 21 Army Group, Tommy was involved in another incident which, as far as I know, has not been recorded. He went absent without leave for three weeks, which was the usual period allowed before the offence became the much more serious one of desertion, and it would have been unthinkable to charge him with desertion. He turned up just in time. When I asked him where he had been, Tommy told me he had gone to Paris, in uniform, and had scoured the city for two Germans who had tortured him before he was sent to Buchenwald. Their faces and their names were inscribed indelibly on his brain and he found out they had been taken prisoner and were being held in police cells.

Tommy pretended he had authority to take the men out for questioning and, through bluff and blustering, he obtained their release. Of course, he made no mention to guards of his personal reason for removing the Nazi sadists from custody and the Germans probably did not recognise him. He would have looked very different, in uniform and well groomed, from the pallid, unshaven wretch they had tortured. He drove them to a quiet corner of the Bois de Boulogne, where he made them get out of the jeep and pumped bullets into their stomachs, leaving them to die where they fell.

Listening to stories of enemy atrocities related by former prisoners and from the people in towns and villages which had been freed from occupation made it difficult for me to control my own emotions when I came across any Germans, whether they were in uniform or not.

I went into Lyon not long after the town had been liberated. Before the German Army left they had lined up British and other prisoners of war, machine-gunned them, then ran tanks over the bodies. That incident was in the forefront of my mind when I sat down in the officers' mess for a meal being served by a German prisoner.

Suddenly I slammed down my knife and fork and heard myself shouting, 'I don't want to see that bloody German in here!'

An SOE agent, Victor Gerson, founder of the famous 'Vic' escape line from Lyon, was present and told me, 'Calm down. The war here is over,' He had probably seen more of the Nazi war crimes than I had and he was right. But I was in no mood to listen to reason.

'No, I'm not going to be served by that bastard,' I said emphatically and I walked out, leaving my untouched meal on the table. It made my stomach turn over to think the German might have been one of those responsible for the shootings, although there was no evidence he was involved.

CHAPTER FIFTEEN

Operation Periwig

As the Allied forces pressed on across Europe we learned of the concern felt by United States security officers about German agents, speaking English with American accents, who had infiltrated the US Army in France. Fortunately most of them were found out before they did much damage. This was about the time the Germans launched their counter-offensive in the Ardennes and we were keen to hit back at them. In the circumstances it seemed strange when SOE received an order to halt any plans for sending agents directly into Germany.

I was at SOE headquarters in Baker Street one day when General (later Field Marshal) Templer called me into his office and said, 'Mandy, from now on there will be no operations into Germany, because the C people think we are a lot of amateurs and decreasing the chances of their men. It's an order – no operations into Germany.' This ban from the Foreign Office (whose secret service chief was known as C) appeared counter-productive and I said, 'But surely, sir, our objective is to tax the German security forces?'

'Yes,' he replied. He then asked me if, during one of my fits of mental diarrhoea I had come up with anything useful, and I put to him a scheme which became known as Operation Periwig.

First of all I enquired of the general if he was familiar with the sayings of Voltaire. He blew a cloud of smoke from his inevitable cigarette, gave me the look of an indulgent uncle who was humouring an exasperating nephew, and he boomed, 'Voltaire? No! Why should I? What has he got to do with it?'

Voltaire, I explained, had said that if God did not exist it would be necessary to invent Him.

'Since our operations into Germany are stopped, why not invent them?' I suggested. 'What about building up an image that we are still dropping people and are continuing our operations, so the

Germans will be chasing their own tails?'

'Damned good idea,' Templer responded enthusiastically.

I promised to work out a scheme and to report back to him, and that was where Flying Officer Ken Potter came in. Potter had been shot down in North Africa and was grounded because of the injuries he sustained. He was a live wire, with some knowledge of German, and he was seconded to SOE as a liaison officer.

He helped me to build up a completely bogus organisation.

Operation Periwig stemmed from my contacts with German prisoners at the Kempton Park POW camp in Surrey. Whenever I interviewed captured SS men they always denied vehemently they were, or ever had been, Nazis. So many sins were covered by the blanket excuse, 'acting under orders'. Through careful questioning, I identified beyond doubt half-a-dozen rabid Nazis and from these selected two who would suit my purpose.

These two SS officers assured me they would do anything to speed the downfall of Adolf Hitler and would work for the Allied cause, if only we would drop them back inside Germany. My plan was to grant their request, but not quite in the way they hoped. To give credence to the deception, I interviewed them again, putting them through a severe grilling before telling them I was satisfied they could be trusted.

They believed I was convinced by their declarations of innocence of war crimes and of their hatred for the Nazis. I briefed them as if they were going on a genuine mission, but in their pockets placed messages in easily-breakable codes, including the names of loyal Nazis, leading members of the Gestapo, who were identified as Allied agents.

The two German 'agents' were flown separately from Tempsford airfield, near Cambridge. One can imagine the thoughts that went through their heads as they passed over the English coast and roared towards Germany – how they had fooled the imbecile British and how they would be welcomed back to the Fatherland when their story was known. I'm certain they had no suspicion their parachutes were defective.

They were dropped at widely different locations over Germany and were picked up dead, the apparent victims of unfortunate accidents. Later on, we received reports that the phoney documents, found on the bodies had caused quite a stir. Gestapo faithful were arrested, protesting the German equivalent 'we've been framed', and Himmler's men were chasing round in circles for months.

Potter's RAF expertise was invaluable during the development of Operation Periwig. We prepared a map with thirty-two target points throughout Germany, close to the fighting areas, and suggested that containers, packed with false information, should be parachuted at these points, ostensibly for our agents but in reality designed to mislead the Gestapo.

Our first approaches to the RAF met with a lukewarm response, but again Ken's contacts came in useful and a number of containers found their way into Nazi hands after the parachutes happened to drift close to German-held positions during supply-dropping missions.

I amused myself for hours in devising simple codes, such as basing a message on every third word from a page in the Bible.

We investigated the possibility of delivering bogus messages by carrier pigeon, but were thwarted by the difficulty of getting hold of German-based birds. Pigeons, of course, return to their own lofts and we could hardly ask the Resistance or the Paras to launch a raid on a pigeon fancier's home in, say, Stuttgart.*

We relied on the arrogance of the Gestapo and their firm belief in the stupidity of the British, even at such a late stage in the war. The Germans really accepted the messages as genuine, delivered into their hands by our incompetence. To give one example: we knew the mayor of a small German town was a member of the Gestapo and I addressed a message to him in the fabricated despatches. He was asked to give shelter to an English agent who would present himself at 11.00 hours on a certain day. This should not be difficult, the message added, in view of the mayor's connection with the Gestapo, and it praised him for operating a 'safe' house. He was arrested and shot. The non-appearance of the agent at eleven o'clock was no doubt attributed to a tip-off. In this episode and in others which resulted from Operation Periwig the

---

*According to other sources, carrier pigeons were dropped, bearing questionnaires for Germans to fill in and return. Some dead pigeons were also said to have been dropped, with the questionnaire completed, in an attempt to make the local population believe their fellow Germans were co-operating with the Allies.

Gestapo obviously thought they had been very clever in liquidating Allied agents with Teutonic efficiency.

I was delighted by the success of this little caper and the deaths of the Nazis had to be weighed against the number of lives saved by keeping the Gestapo otherwise engaged.

Of course, the support of General Templer opened doors for us. Success and Templer were synonymous. In 1942, at the age of 44, he had been the youngest lieutenant-general in the Army. At his own request he stepped down in rank from corps commander so he could command a division in the field as a major-general, in which capacity he served at Anzio. Fate dealt him a cruel blow in Italy, where he became the only general in military history to have been almost killed by a piano on active service. It happened when he was leading the 6th Armoured Division against the Gothic Line, during the advance on Rome in 1944. As Templer was rushing towards the battle in a jeep, the road was barred by a 15 cwt truck carrying a piano. Templer's driver gave a blast on the jeep's horn, the lorry turned off the road and on to a landmine and the piano was blown on top of Templer. It broke his back and, after surgery in Naples, he was invalided home.

For most men, such an incident would have been the end of any further part in the war. But Templer fought his way back to health and later the same year was in uniform again, helping to organise the espionage and guerilla campaign against Germany.

When I first met him I was immediately struck by the force of his personality. He was a slim, elegant man, with a neat moustache, and he had the clipped, incisive way of speaking which often marks a high-ranking officer. Due to the accident, he had to wear a surgical collar for months and was left with a pronounced limp, which was offset by his military bearing, a credit to his Sandhurst training.

It was easy to be misled by Templer's charm. His demeanour often *appeared* to be easy-going, but he was really as tough and unyielding as a pair of brand new Army boots. On the day he arrived at SOE headquarters he called the officers together and spoke to us informally.

'I'm the new boy here,' he said. 'You know the game – I don't. I have a great deal to learn and I shall be guided by you chaps. After all, I'm only a regular soldier.'

We must have seemed a very strange and unconventional bunch to that most conventional of Army officers. He listened attentively as each of us described our roles. The next day we were surprised how much information he had absorbed in so short a time and he made it very clear he was our boss, although Gubbins retained overall command. I was Templer's staff officer for four months while he was assisting SOE and recovering his strength.

Templer ordered me, as head of the Russian section, to liaise with General Koenig, a friend of de Gaulle's, who had assumed command of all Resistance efforts in France through the newly-formed *État-Major des Forces Françaises de l'Interior* (EMFFI).

Koenig and his Resistance sources were able to give us an assessment of the numbers of Russians who were in France with the German Army. These included the Caucasian Cavalry Division, who came over to us without much persuasion. They were considered first-rate people, basically devoted to Russia but very anti-Bolshevik and also anti-Nazi.

Usually on such missions I assumed the rank of lieutenant-colonel. On my first visit to Koenig, however, I was given a Movement Order designating my rank as acting major. This made me rather indignant, not only because it hurt my pride but also because the higher rank made it easier for me to obtain information and to negotiate with more senior officers on level terms

I tackled Templer about it, as I thought there might have been an oversight.

'With respect, General, what is going on?' I said. 'You know I'm always kicked up in rank on these trips.'

He regarded me sourly, obviously far from impressed.

'Not on your life, Mandy. You'll bloody well go out as a second lieutenant if I say so. Your rank does not matter. You are representing me, Major-General Templer, and you carry the authority of my rank when you speak to the French.'

'All right, sir,' I answered meekly. 'Orders are orders.'

I had my meeting with Koenig, who held the rank of lieutenant-general. On my return I marched into Templer's office with a smirk on my face.

'By the way, sir,' I said, 'I suggest that you ought to have stood up when I came in.'

He blinked. 'I beg your pardon? Are you talking to me? What the hell do you mean?'

'Well, sir, you said my rank doesn't matter; that I carry the authority of the person I represent. I am here as a representative of the French Commander, with the authority of Lieutenant-General Koenig, and with a message from him that reads, 'Will you inform Major-General Templer on my behalf . . .'

Templer let me get no further and wasted no words. 'Piss off,' he muttered as he snatched the paper from my hand.

Our paths crossed many times in the closing stages of the war and in the years after the German surrender. Templer joined Field Marshal Montgomery's GHQ early in 1945 as Director of Civil Affairs and he became Military Governor of the British Zone. He later achieved great success as High Commissioner in Malaya and reached the top of the ladder as Field Marshal Sir Gerald Templer, Chief of the Imperial General Staff.

Perhaps my favourite story of Templer's period in Germany concerned his part in the occupation of Cologne. Monty's 21 Army Group had barely had time to cross the Rhine and secure the ancient cathedral city before Templer surveyed the desolation and decided to evict the elderly mayor from the Town Hall, in favour of a younger man. That old and 'inefficient' mayor turned out to be Dr Konrad Adenauer, the future Chancellor of Western Germany. Templer was forever after known in Germany as the man who sacked Adenauer.

Despite his fastidious nature and an aesthetic appearance, Templer could be wickedly crude in his language, which he sprinkled with barrack-room expletives, particularly when faced with the informal attitudes of SOE operatives. Once, when I was Night Duty Officer at Baker Street, he called me into his office in the early hours and I dashed up the stairs as I was, in shirt sleeves and braces, without my tunic. He bit hard on his cigarette holder as I walked in and snapped, 'You bloody well get back to your room and come here properly dressed.'

So I went downstairs again and, ignoring the battledress tunic slung across a chair, I got out my best uniform, including the hat, Sam Browne belt and swagger stick. Back up to Templer's office I clattered. I rapped on his door and, stepping smartly inside, I gave the general a spanking salute, exclaiming, 'Sir!' at the same time.

'Well, Mandy. That's much better,' he commented. 'I shall make a fucking soldier out of you yet.'

'Excuse me, General,' I said. 'With all respect to your rank, I stand a much better chance of making a fucking civilian out of you than you do of making a soldier out of me.'

'Get out of my office,' he barked, but there was a twinkle in his eyes.

Years later, when he was no longer active in the Army and had become a director of an insurance firm, the first of a number of company directorships he held, I sent a letter to him: 'My dear Field Marshal. I succeeded – you failed. You are a civilian, but you never made a soldier out of me.'

Templer had a wonderful wife, the personification of everything a senior officer's lady should be. And whenever I saw them in private I was embarrassed by the language he used in her presence. Like most of the best British generals, Templer was of Irish extraction, which may have accounted for his directness of speech.

CHAPTER SIXTEEN

The Betrayal

The affair of the enforced return of Russian prisoners, condemning more than two million people to execution or the living death of Soviet labour camps, was in my submission one of the most horrible and despicable episodes in British history. Some measure of the shame felt by those responsible can be gleaned from the way in which the details of that crime against humanity were kept a close secret for two-and-a-half decades. In fact not until files were opened under the thirty-year rule did much of the information become public knowledge.

Alexander Solzhenitsyn, in *The Gulag Archipelago*, wrote:

It is surprising that in the West, where political secrets cannot be kept long, since they inevitably come out in print or are disclosed, the secret of *this* particular act of betrayal has been very well and carefully kept by the British and American governments. This is truly the last secret, or one of the last, of the Second World War. Having often encountered these people in camps, I was unable to believe for a whole quarter-century that the public in the West knew *nothing* of this action of the Western governments, this massive handing over of ordinary Russian people to retribution and death.

It was Solzhenitsyn's book which, in 1974, forced examination of the repatriation of the Russians against their will from prison camps in the West. In the same year Nicholas Bethell published *The Last Secret*, and three years later Nikolai Tolstoy's book, *Victims of Yalta*, contained new information and caused a further storm of protest and indignation.

As I have indicated, the dilemma of the Russians who joined the German Army, or followed General Vlasov, and of those who were either enslaved or imprisoned in concentration camps, was known about before the Allies landed in France. But the extent of the problem did not become clear until very much later.

The official Moscow line had been to pretend the situation did not exist. As Stalin would have it, there were no Russian prisoners in German hands, only Russian traitors, since in his view any man who allowed himself to be captured and did not die for the Motherland was a traitor. Thus, he refused to co-operate with the International Red Cross in the sending of parcels to prisoners. As for the Cossacks and others who served alongside the Germans in the mistaken belief that they might help to defeat the Bolsheviks, or merely to save their own lives, they were worse than vermin as far as the Soviet government was concerned and, like vermin, they must be exterminated as quickly as possible. A third factor was the thousands of Russians of all ages – men, women and children – who had fled from Bolshevik tyranny or who had been engulfed during the German Operation Barbarossa invasion and who had been forced to work as slave labour for the Nazis. Strictly speaking, a large proportion were not even Soviet citizens, because they, or their parents, had left Russia before the Soviet Union was established, or else they were from the Baltic States and other annexed areas.

Stalin had an unspoken fear, which was probably the real reason for his determination to eliminate millions of Russian exiles. He kept control by terror and ignorance and did not want any Russians, White or otherwise, to have an opportunity of spreading Western ideas within the USSR, particularly as it would be difficult to explain why about a million of them preferred to throw in their lot with Hitler in an attempt to overthrow the Communists.

After the invasion of Italy and the landings in Normandy, we gradually became aware that the number of Russians who had been separated from their homeland was far greater than we had anticipated. But all estimates made by people directly involved, like myself, were hopelessly wrong, for we had no way of finding out the truth. It became a political matter and the politicians maintained a conspiracy of silence. That situation did not change with the passage of years. Even today, surviving political figures who had some role in the repatriation betrayal refuse to talk about it, still less to explain their motives. Estimates in recent years have put the number of Russians involved at more than two million and possible as high as four million. Not all of them reached the labour camps or faced the firing squads, for many committed suicide rather than go back.

Much of the blame for the tragedy could be attributed to a mixture of naivity and political expediency. It has been said that, in those closing months of the war, the Soviet Union's word was still trusted as our honoured comrade-in-arms. Yet one had only to look at recent history to realise the true nature of the beast. If the repression, the internments without trial, the labour camps and the devastation of areas such as the Ukraine were not enough, then the rape of the Baltic States and the swallowing up of Poland ought to have provided sufficient warning.

Roosevelt was a sick man at Yalta, when the prisoners' fate was settled, and he and Churchill were completely outmanoeuvred by Stalin, who obtained everything he wanted from that conference. But the groundwork for the great betrayal had been laid some months earlier, in Moscow during October 1944, when Eden agreed to the return of Russian prisoners. The agreement was expanded and signed at Yalta the following February and was confirmed at the Potsdam Conference in July 1945, during which Attlee replaced Churchill as Prime Minister and by which time Roosevelt was dead.

An argument advanced to explain the British Government's stance was the claim that, if the Russians were not repatriated by force, Stalin would vent his spite on the Britons and Americans who were held in German prisoner of war camps over-run by the Soviet advance. To my mind it was not a very strong argument. What would Stalin have done to those Allied troops? Shoot them? Send them to Siberia? At worst, it seemed to me, he would have delayed their return home, on the face of it a small price to pay when set against the carnage which befell the Russian prisoners. The Foreign Office were more concerned to keep up the pretence of cordial Anglo-Soviet relations, which they clearly rated more highly than the prisoners' lives. And there was the exaggerated difficulty of absorbing into Western nations the millions of displaced persons.

Among the first of the Russian prisoners I met were some who had been snatched during raids on France ahead of D-Day. They confirmed that large numbers of Russians were being sent, under

German command, to man the coastline of France, the Atlantic Wall.

Within days of the Normandy invasion I interrogated several batches of Russian prisoners who had been forced to fight on the German side. My approach was a simple one: if they were taken prisoner in German Army uniforms, with German paybooks, they were, as far as I was concerned, Germans and should be treated as such under the Geneva Convention. This view was opposed by officials from the Foreign Office, who were not swayed by my assertion that if one applied to all nations the criteria which they were applying to the Russians, then half the American Army should be sent back to Poland, Italy and Puerto Rico.

One bright spot was the support I received from Lord Selborne who, as Minister of Economic Warfare, had responsibility for SOE. He reacted quickly and sympathetically when I told him of my fears for the safety of the prisoners and of my conviction, after countless hours of talking with them, that the agreement sought by Stalin amounted to a death warrant.

A compassionate man, he was horrified when I described to him how the Russians I had interviewed had been recruited into the German forces. They were starved, three to four weeks without food or water, until they were in some cases reduced to cannibalism. They drank urine and licked condensation off walls. After this, they were lined up and a German officer asked, 'Who wants to join Vlasov's Army to fight on the German side?' There was no response.

The next order was, 'Every tenth man take one step forward.' And those men were shot. It was hardly surprising most of the survivors put on German uniforms. Once they were in the Army they were told by German officers they would be executed as traitors by the Allies if they were taken prisoner or if they surrendered. (The leaflets we had distributed among the Russians promised they would not be shot if they surrendered and stated they would be treated in just the same way as any combatants. The leaflets urged the Russians to give themselves up and added, 'It is not your war.' Whoever framed the message ought to have been jailed for false representation.)

My first report about the prisoners had gone to Gubbins, who instructed me to write a detailed letter, which he signed and sent to the minister, Selborne. Within a day or two Gubbins told me

Selborne wanted to hear my report at first hand and I was to go to his office. The Foreign Office had given Selborne a cock-and-bull story, maintaining that most of the prisoners were eager to go back to Russia. During our interview I convinced him of the truth of my report and in July 1944 he wrote to Anthony Eden, the Foreign Secretary, opposing a Cabinet decision to repatriate to the Soviet Union all Russian prisoners who had served in the German Army. Selborne asked for Eden's backing and in this letter, and in a later letter to Winston Churchill, he referred to the interviews I had conducted with forty-five prisoners from three camps.

Lord Selborne's letter to Eden contained the passage:

> As you may know, one of my officers has during the past four weeks interviewed a number of Russian prisoners and in every case their story is substantially the same.
>
> In the first place they were subject to incredible hardship and treatment on being taken prisoner. They were marched in many cases for several days without food. They were placed in concentration camps under appalling sanitary conditions and were starved. They became infested with vermin, they were the victims of loathsome diseases, and starvation was carried to such a point that cannibalism became prevalent. In more than one instance, the Germans filmed cannibalistic meals for propaganda purposes.

Selborne's letter to Churchill was in the same vein and he pointed out to the Prime Minister, 'None of them have any doubt that if they are sent back to Russia they will be shot and their families disgraced and maltreated.'

Eden's reaction was to write on Selborne's letter:

> It does not deal with the point. If these men do not go back to Russia, where can they go? We don't want them here.

In fact Selborne had suggested the prisoners might be absorbed in under-populated countries, 'if their number is not too great.' He referred to the possibility that France would give political asylum to Russians who offered to join the Foreign Legion or to settle in

French colonies such as Madagascar. There were other possibilities. Through my own enquiries I established that Paraguay would be willing to take 200,000 Russian exiles to develop the cultivation of castor beans.

Churchill was inclined to use 'all the apparatus of delay' in an attempt to help the prisoners. But Eden, while acknowledging that many of the Russians 'must have suffered terribly', was nonetheless insistent that Britain could not be 'permanently saddled' with them. He also used to good effect his strongest argument: to refuse to hand over the prisoners might harm Anglo-Soviet relations and the Soviet Government might create difficulties over the return of Allied prisoners from camps in Poland and eastern Germany.

In September, Eden reported to the Cabinet, saying the number of Soviet prisoners in Britain was 3,750 and, although he believed some of them would face execution in Russia, he was still convinced they should be returned. The number of prisoners mentioned by Eden was, of course, the tip of the iceberg. In fairness, it is not clear whether or not Eden realised the full extent of the problem. Advice which Eden received from the Foreign Office was far from sound. Much of it came from Christopher Warner, head of the Northern Department and thus responsible for the Soviet desk at the Foreign Office, who analysed Lord Selborne's letter. Warner claimed, among other things, that most of the Russian prisoners at Kempton park wished to go 'home' and he ignored my observation that such statements were influenced by misleading information and by the presence of an NKVD agent in the prisoners' midst.

I went to the Foreign Office and had a blazing row with Warner, which ended in him banging his desk and shouting at me to get out of his office. He accused me of lying and said my report was not objective. I said the trouble was it was *too* objective for him and contained too many unpalatable truths. He made an official complaint about my conduct, which Selborne and Gubbins rejected. And in a sarcastic memorandum, Warner wrote:

I know the SOE officer who provided the first report and he has been in touch with this department. I doubt whether he is the right person to carry out an objective interrogation. He is a Russian-speaking Balt and does not make the impression of being trained at sifting evidence.

According to Lord Bethell, 'The absurdity of this comment was revealed with the passing of time.' In a 1974 article in *The Times*, he wrote:

> Warner was certainly wrong, both about the letter and about Manderstam. No one seriously believes now that the Russian prisoners were exaggerating either about their sufferings in Germany or about the fate that awaited them in Russia. And Manderstam ... succeeded in building up a chemical engineering business (sic) worth many millions of pounds, thus proving surely that he was capable of being objective and of sifting evidence. Also his master, Anthony Eden, had far more political influence than Selborne.

Ironically, some of the advice and comment on the prisoners which percolated up from the lower ranks at the Foreign Office came from the Soviet agents Donald Maclean and Guy Burgess. And in 1944 Kim Philby, the other member of the triumvirate, had been put in charge of a new section designed to operate against communism and the Soviet Union.

Sir James Grigg, Secretary of State of War, apparently agreed with my assessment of the situation, as detailed by Lord Selborne, but he referred to the danger that the Russians 'may not be ready to co-operate in sending back speedily to us the British and other Allied prisoners who fall into their hands.' He went on, 'Obviously our public opinion would bitterly resent any delay in getting our men home, or any infliction of unnecessary hardship on them, and if the choice is between hardship to our men and death to the Russians our choice is plain.'

With such arguments was sealed the fate of millions of Russians.

CHAPTER SEVENTEEN

Yalta's Aftermath

Our leaders had reached a decision which we in the field were ordered to carry out, no matter how distasteful we felt it to be. As is the way with war, the chairborne brigade who drafted their elegant minutes, sipped their Whitehall tea and ambled through St James's Park before an evening bottle or two of claret did not need to bother their heads or dirty their hands with the results of their deliberations. They did not see the faces of thousands of Russians who were shoved aboard cattle trucks, nor did they see the bodies of the men, women and children who died rather than go back.

The lucky ones had guns to end their lives. Many hanged themselves, others jumped in front of trains, or used knives and razors to slash their own throats and arteries, and some threw themselves from bridges. Fathers and mothers killed their children and then committed suicide.

I may have been the first, but I was by no means the only officer to protest and to see the implications of the repatriation policy. A number of high-ranking British and American officers voiced their disapproval – notably on the British side Alexander and Montgomery – and some took positive action.

Two generals described, in letters to *The Times*, how they followed Nelson's example in turning a blind eye to a political decision.

General Sir Horatius Murray was commanding the 6th Armoured Division in the general area of Villach, Klagenfurt, when they captured a number of formations, including Cossacks, and then received orders that all Russian POWs were to be repatriated.

I called a conference of the senior officers concerned, informed them of the orders I had received, but told them I did not intend to give effect to them immediately, and that, in the meantime, they should consider their positions and convey this to all ranks.

We had remarkably few prisoners on our hands the following day.
They melted into the hinterland with no difficulty at all.

Major General Sir Alec Bishop explained, '...we did succeed in
preventing the repatriation against their will of large numbers of
Baltic (Latvian, Lithuanian and Estonian) citizens and Poles,
despite great pressure from the Soviet authorities.'

He gave credit to a number of British civil and military officers
serving in Germany, 'who resolutely opposed the return of these
people against their clearly, and often passionately, expressed will'.

An American view was given by General Walter Bedell Smith,
General Eisenhower's Chief of Staff in North Africa and Western
Europe, who became US Ambassador to Moscow.

In his book *Moscow Mission*, Bedell Smith described the agreement
made at Yalta and reaffirmed at Potsdam, concerning the return of
displaced persons, as 'our most serious problem with the Soviet
Government while I was in Germany'. Soviet and American
interpretations of the Yalta agreement differed considerably, he
pointed out:

> We believed that we were talking about facilitating the return to
> Russia of those Soviet nationals who desired to return, plus, of
> course, such individuals as might be charged specifically with war
> crimes. We certainly did not intend to violate the traditional
> American attitude toward giving sanctuary to political refugees,
> of whom we found thousands in Germany. Many of these were
> from the Baltic States, which had been incorporated into the
> Soviet Union since the war began, and others from those parts of
> Poland and Rumania which had recently been annexed by the
> Russians.

Bedell Smith found a 'somewhat overzealous' American unit which
had begun forcibly to load on to a train some of the Russian
displaced persons who had refused to return voluntarily to the Soviet
Union:

> Some of them had taken refuge in a church and pleaded with the
> Americans not to send them back to the Soviet Union. When their

(*top left*) Major General Templer, left, with General Mark Clark in November, 1943 in Italy.

(*top right*) General Alexander chatting with General de Gaulle, North Africa, 24 June 1943.

Bodies of Russian slave workers being recovered from a basement which had been deliberately set ablaze by a German policeman near Osnabruck, April 1945.

Russian ex-prisoners attack a Nazi who shot two Russian slaves.

(*Top left*) Cossacks on parade, serving with the German forces. (*Centre left*) Cossacks surrendering their arms. (*Centre right*) A leaflet which tells Russia[n]s serving with the Germans that th[ey] will get fair treatment. (*Bottom le[ft]*) A group of liberated Russians at Stalag XIB, 14 April 1945. (*Botto[m] right*) A half-starved Russian lim[ps] out of a German concentration camp.

Ваши немецкие оф[и]церы говорят вам что [вы] будете растрелены ес[ли] вы сдадитесь или взя[ты] в плен.

ЭТО НЕПРАВДА

Союзная армия отн[о]сится к иностранцам [в] немецкой армии точ[но] также как к друг[им] воюющим солдатам, понятно, согласно [с] международными пра[ви]лами ведения войны.

Это не ваша война

Приготовьте се[бя] сдаться при перв[ой] возможности.

pleas seemed unavailing, one or two actually committed suicide.

He said instructions were issued immediately to the US troops that no one was to be repatriated forcibly, except war criminals, Of course, the situation was not entirely resolved by the order, although I must say, compared with the British, the Americans emerged with greater credit.

My own worst fears received confirmation from a Guards officer who was aboard a ship which took prisoners to Archangel. He told me Soviet secret police agents had infiltrated the ship, posing as prisoners. When they reached the Russian port, the agents had already categorised the prisoners, who were informed, 'You're going to Siberia .... You're going to be shot.' Many were slaughtered within minutes of being taken ashore. The officer said it was a 'terrible business' and he heard the sound of machine guns all night. I remember him clearly because he was only about five feet two inches tall, the smallest Guards officer I ever saw.

I resolved to save the lives of at least forty Russians who had served with Vlasov's Army by training them for SOE missions behind German lines. A high percentage of the German slave labour force consisted of Russians and I believed forty trained soldiers would cause untold damage if we dropped them in Germany with the aim of linking up with their fellow countrymen in factories and organising sabotage and subversion. In my judgement, a tremendous impact would be caused in Germany by such a party of Russians arriving from England with promises of fair treatment for their compatriots.

The members of my team were selected from prisoners I interrogated at Kempton Park. I supervised their training, selected NCOs and organised a parachute course at Ringway Airfield. We could not find suitable uniforms, so I got my tailor to turn Army issue tunics and trousers into forty made-to-measure uniforms at my own expense. The uniforms and new sense of purpose gave the dejected Russians a fillip. They were superb. Air Vice Marshal Critchley inspected them during a visit to Kempton Park and said to me, 'The Brigade of Guards could not have turned out a better outfit than you have.'

My Russians had all held commissions or had been NCOs in Vlasov's Army and they were determined to succeed in their missions. When we were going through the parachute training at Ringway one of them grabbed my wrist and said, 'By the way, sir, I will not have the guts to jump. You must promise to push me and, if I hold on to the rim of the jumping hole, tread on my fingers.' When his turn came to slip from a platform beneath a tethered balloon, he froze and I had to shove him. He was terrified, but I was frightened myself when I made my first parachute descent. We all found the balloon jumps to be far more unnerving than plunging from an aircraft.

We had a group of 'safe' houses in the Kempton Park area, where the Russians lived during their training. The first mission, using four men, was all set up and ready to go when I was informed by General Gubbins that we must obtain Foreign Office consent. There was a further complication: SOE and the NKVD had reciprocal missions in Moscow and London. Our man in Moscow was a shady character, Brigadier George Hill, who must have been consulted by the Foreign Office and who sent a message, saying clearance from the Soviet representatives was imperative before we went any further.

This gave me no choice but to approach the head of the NKVD Mission in London, Colonel Ivan Chichaev, who said he would pass my request to Moscow, which in all probability meant the chief of the Soviet secret police and spy networks, L.P. Beria. The next I knew, after a lapse of several weeks, was a stern warning from our Foreign Office not to proceed with the operation.

I was furious and, completely against all the rules of protocol, I sent a signal to Brigadier Hill, whom I blamed for this turn of events. If the NKVD had been looking for an efficient representative they could not have found a better one than him, I told Hill.

Gubbins tore a strip off me when he heard about it. 'You can't do that sort of thing,' he said. 'I understand how you feel, and to some extent I agree with you, but you should know better.'

Hill, during a visit to London, confirmed he had used his influence to stop my Russian parachutists. He sent for me and said with a sneer, 'So you are Manderstam. If there is one man I would like to see shot at dawn it's you.'

I told him the feeling was fully reciprocated.

I made it clear I thought he was taking the Foreign Office for a ride and we parted the best of enemies. He had tremendous self-conceit, but I was not impressed by the colourful stories he told, starting with his childhood as the son of a merchant who traded in the Baltic States, St Petersburg and Moscow and who went to the Nizhni Novgorod fair, just as my own father had done. The yarns Hill related about his career as a British spy in Russia during the rise of Bolshevism made him sound like a cross between James Bond and a Boy's Own Paper hero, with a dash of Valentino. Yet he was the most unlikely looking man of action, a little over five feet tall and almost as broad.

He referred to himself as being 'a legend' in Russia and told in graphic detail how, among other things, he saved the Rumanian royal jewels; how he waded a freezing river into Russia to blow up a bridge when no one else would do the job; how he saved a lovely Jewess from the Soviet secret police by hiding her in his bathroom. And how he diced with death and turned the tables on would-be assassins, once by a thrust from his swordstick and another time by deft use of a brick.

I was sure George Hill was a triple agent. There was, in my opinion, no other explanation for his conduct and for subsequent events other than that he was feeding information to the British, the Russians and the Germans. Even when he was liaising with the NKVD on an official basis, I believe Hill supplied to them a great deal of important information and received little in return. He had been promoted to the control of SOE's Mission in Moscow through his pre-war connections with the SIS and helped by the grandiose claims which he made for himself. Some of these exploits involved the spy Sidney Reilly and the official British agent in Moscow, Bruce Lockhart.

Kim Philby referred to Hill, in *My Silent War*, as 'jolly George Hill', and added:

Immensely paunchy, he looked rather like Soglow's king with a bald pate instead of a crown. he was later appointed head of the SOE Mission in Moscow, where the Russians hailed him with delight. They knew all about him. A very belated security check of his conference room in Moscow revealed a fearsome number of sources of leakage.

There was an occasion when Hill asked for a £20,000 diamond, which he said he needed to bribe a woman NKVD agent who lived with him. Gubbins asked my opinion and I said, 'The whole thing is damned phoney. No NKVD girl would be his mistress unless she was getting some really good information from him.'

Our ambassador, Sir Archibald Clark Kerr, appeared to be completely taken in by Hill and gave his seal of approval with the words, 'Whatever Brigadier Hill says, goes.'

I was suspicious of Hill's motive in asking for the diamond and I strongly suspected no valuable information would come our way through its disposal. It seemed obvious the Soviet Mata Hari was milking him instead of him milking her. Colonel Benham took me with him to Hatton Garden to choose the diamond, which was despatched to Hill, despite my opposition, and we heard no more of it.

Perhaps significantly, Hill was one of the very few British officers, to my knowledge, who obtained a top job immediately after the war with a German company. He was appointed managing director of a mineral water firm and three years later he was awarded the German Order of Merit for services to the country's industry.

Hill tried his best to discredit me, aided by Christopher Warner, and they might have succeeded if General Gubbins had not been such a loyal friend. When Warner telephoned him from the Foreign Office and said, 'Get rid of this man Manderstam,' Gubbins replied, 'If you want to get rid of Manderstam, you can have my resignation at the same time.'

Ivan Chichaev and I also had a friendly, if guarded, relationship. The analogy of a game of chess is often used to describe negotiations with Soviet representatives and that was how it was whenever I met Chichaev. He would make a move. I made a counter-move. We each conceded a pawn or two and the exchanges invariably ended in stalemate.

Our negotiations over the forty Russians were typical. Some time after the operation into Germany had been aborted, Chichaev asked if he could be allowed to interview the men. I pointed out that his own superiors had torpedoed the plan and there seemed little to be gained from his proposed interview. In any case, the men would be returned to the POW camp, where he could apply through the normal channels to see them.

As that move had not produced the desired result, Chichaev probed down another flank. Could I give him a list of our 'toys', the special devices used by SOE agents, which Brigadier Hill had promised to him? These 'toys' included gas pistols, pencil guns and a poison which gave the symptoms of syphilis which, as I have mentioned, I had once considered using to kill a German officer. Fine, I told Chichaev, but could I have a similar list of the NKVD's toys? He said he would need clearance from Moscow. 'All right,' I replied. 'Get me the clearance in writing and we will be in business.'

'That's an insult,' he protested. 'Why in writing? I give my word of honour. No one has ever doubted my word.'

Despite his assurances that he wanted to co-operate he did not produce a list and so he did not receive ours, at least not from me.

Referring to my dealings with Chichaev, Nikolai Tolstoy wrote, in *Victims of Yalta*:

This interview might well have been taken as a model of how to conduct negotiations with the Soviets. Whilst the NKVD had successfully blocked British proposals, Manderstam had conceded nothing on his side. There had been no recriminations, and indeed Chichaev went out of his way to express his friendship for Manderstam. The statesmen of Yalta and Potsdam might have learned much by pondering the implications of this exchange..

Chichaev was an exception. Working with him at the NKVD Mission was Major Krasinski, a hard-line Bolshevik whom I detested. An opportunity for me to take him down a peg occurred when I was asked to liaise with Krasinski and to act as an escort for him to Southampton, on his way to Italy and the Balkans. I signalled to Southampton to expect Major-*General* Krasinski, who should be afforded every facility, and I made sure a copy reached Krasinski's superiors, who believed he had initiated the message. As a result he was involved in a terrific row and Moscow asked him for a full explanation. It was a cardinal offence for a Russian officer to misrepresent his rank.

*

Nothing gave me greater pleasure during the war than the disappearance of my forty Russian parachutists from the Kempton Park POW camp. I put off Chichaev for as long as possible, but we reached a point when his visit to the prisoners could be delayed no further. When I told them Chichaev was on the way and they were all destined to be transported to Russia, they shook their heads and vowed they would never go back.

The depths of despair to which these fine men had sunk was impressed on me most forcibly during a series of interviews. One of the Russian prisoners, a Dr Petrowsky, who had been a medical officer in the Red Army before he joined Vlasov, was particularly upset. He came to see me in my room, which was on the third floor of a requisitioned house. It was a warm day, the windows were wide open and I could hear the sounds of children playing in the street far below.

Petrowsky's face was white and set and his hand trembled as he reached for the cup of coffee I offered to him.

'Are you afraid the Soviets will shoot you?' I asked.

'No,' he said firmly, 'I am not afraid for myself. You see I am a hero back home. Everyone thinks I was killed fighting in the Russian Army. If I go back they will take it out on my parents, on my brother and my sister. The whole family will be penalised.'

He pleaded with me to find a way for him to avoid being in the next batch of prisoners to be handed over to the Russians.

'There is no sure way,' I replied. 'Unless you break your legs and land in hospital. . .'

I had barely completed the sentence before Petrowsky rose from his chair, took three or four paces, and jumped to the concrete thirty feet beneath my window. He was picked up with severe fractures of both legs and broken ribs. His act of desperation helped to crystalise the thoughts running through my head and heightened my determination not to allow the men in my specially-trained team to be handed over to the Russian authorities. But my move had to be made before Chichaev had had a chance to interrogate them, or to arrange their removal from the camp.

Even now I refuse to disclose how the prisoners 'disappeared' and where they went and I have quite deliberately avoided contact with any of them, for the Soviet secret police has a long memory. Suffice it to say that on the morning of Chichaev's visit a British officer, Major Phillips, who spoke Russian but declined to admit the fact, came to me, drew himself to attention, and said, 'I am sorry to report, sir, forty prisoners have escaped.' And we both sported broad smiles for the rest of the morning.

Chichaev nearly had a heart attack.

'It's you, Manderstam. You did it. I'll report you for this.'

'All right,' I replied. 'Go and see the general.'

He did, and he told Gubbins, 'Manderstam engineered the escape of forty prisoners to prevent me interviewing them.'

Gubbins put on his best display of indignation. 'How dare you accuse one of my officers! What evidence have you got? I can assure you we do not go in for that sort of thing.'

Chichaev, when he calmed down, accepted the episode as just another nuance in the fortunes of war. We remained on friendly terms and, as a gesture of goodwill, I took him to the theatre to see a performance of James Bridie's comedy *Storm in a Teacup*, which was made into a film starring Rex Harrison and Vivien Leigh. The sophisticated dialogue completely flummoxed the Russian. 'Where is the moral?' he kept asking, as he could not understand how Westerners could go to a theatre or cinema merely to be entertained and not instructed.

Chichaev was also perplexed by the way in which I was able to contradict the official line, especially as the Foreign Office appeared to be intent on pleasing the Russians at all costs. He protested to Gubbins, 'Manderstam is a nice person, but he argues too much. If you would order him not to argue with me, then he would be a really first rate man.' Gubbins laughed, but otherwise paid no attention to the request. He and Chichaev got on well together, socially, and Gubbins gave a party in Chichaev's honour.

Although he was born in Tokyo, Gubbins was of Scottish descent and like a typical Scotsman believed he could out-drink anyone. Chichaev, being a Russian, was of a similar mind. So they began to match each other, drink for drink, mixing vodka, whisky, gin and wine, while the rest of us watched. In the interests of truth I must record that the Russian won. He was still standing, albeit with a silly grin on his face and swaying a little, while our leader was slumped at the table.

I have not seen Chichaev since the war and I have had only one, indirect, greeting from him. He was attached for a time to the Russian embassy in Prague, where he met Perkins, the former head of SOE's Polish Section, who had joined the Foreign Office. The Russian asked Perkins how I was getting on and sent his best wishes. Chichaev, if he is still alive, may well be active still within the KGB, as the Russians have no age limit for their officers or political leaders.

One must never forget, in dealing with Russians, that they have a completely different sense of values. For instance, I remember speaking to Chichaev on the subject of strikes. 'We do not have strikes,' he said. And when I asked why, he replied, 'Because the industry belongs to the State. Whoever goes on strike is guilty of sabotaging industry and he is shot.' Such a simple solution would hardly appeal to Western trades unions, I commented.

There was an occasion when Chichaev invited me to defect. 'My friend, you are only a major,' he said to me. 'If you come over to us you will be a full general, I promise you.'

'Where – in the Lubianka? And how long will it last, twenty-four hours?'

'I give my word of honour.'

I told him not to take me for a fool.

He could be an agreeable companion. An ex-Tsarist officer, from the equivalent of the Brigade of Guards, he went over to the Bolsheviks when the revolution broke out in 1917 and he genuinely believed in Communism. I did not tell him I, too, had done service in the Red Army. In fact, despite his gentle probing, I was careful not to reveal any details of my links with Soviet Russia. For one thing, my brother Benjamin was still there. The only time I relaxed my guard was shortly after the war when I wrote to my brother, who was a leading solicitor in Riga, and enclosed a photograph of myself in uniform. I was stupid enough to believe, since we had been fighting on the same side and had won a great victory, that no harm would be done by resuming contact with my brother. The letter was opened and Benjamin was interrogated for days about its contents and about his British officer brother. As a result, he was deprived of the right to practise for two years. He was in dire straits, unable to earn a living. I sent him money, through friends, and I managed to get him out. Benjamin settled in Canada, a small fish in a big pond, whereas in Riga he had been a big fish in a small pond. What made it worse was the fact that, although a brilliant man, he spoke little English. There is limited use for a lawyer who cannot communicate.*

I almost ended up in Russia myself towards the end of the war, when Gubbins, with Selborne's support, recommended me to be head of SOE's Moscow Mission in succession to George Hill. We were not informed why Hill was leaving Moscow, the most likely reason being that he had done his worst and had lost interest.

Once again the dark shadow of the Foreign Office fell across my path and my appointment was vetoed: 'We are not going to send *this* man to Moscow.'

The fact that I knew the Russians as well, if not better, than anyone else in SOE was of no account. There were too many blots on my copybook.

Instead they sent Colonel Anthony Benham who had been a regular soldier, who spoke no Russian and who had a drink problem. I had known Benham since my first day with SOE and liked him very much. We remained friends, and in his will he left me his desk, which now stands in my London office. The Moscow posting was a disaster for him. He suffered badly from phlebitis and, with duty free liquor on tap at the Embassy, he drank himself silly. He died within a short time of his return to London after spending only about eight months in Moscow.

* Benjamin's death, in Canada, on 4 September 1984 was a tremendous shock to his brother, who survived him by a mere twelve weeks. RH.

CHAPTER EIGHTEEN

Berlin Encounter

After the Soviet Army had taken Berlin I was sent there to interrogate Russian-speaking refugees and prisoners. The Allies had been kept waiting outside the German capital and the scenes which met our eyes when we were eventually allowed in were incredible. Not only were the buildings devastated, the people were crushed as well. In the first days of the onslaught the Russians had pushed to the front their Mongol troops, who were absolute savages. They roamed the streets like mad dogs, killing indiscriminately and raping any woman they came across, no matter what their age or condition. This was done deliberately to avenge the atrocities committed by the German invaders of Russia and to stamp out any resistance by the civilian population. Following the Mongols came the crack regiments from Siberia, whose behaviour was exemplary.

I knew Berlin well in pre-war days but now I had difficulty finding my way around because mountains of rubble and ragged, fire-blackened sections of walls were all that was left of once familiar buildings. Coffee, cigarettes and pieces of soap became forms of currency in the ravaged city and it was a chastening experience to see cultured women and girls of school age prostituting themselves for such items.

Strictly speaking, we were not allowed to fraternise with the Germans, but I had a friend called Pfender in Berlin and I was determined to see him. I was staying at the Savoy Hotel, Fasenenstrasse, close to the Zoological gardens, or rather the bomb and shell-blasted remains of the zoo, and the last address I had for Pfender was some distance away in the French Zone. I sent a message, asking him to join me at the hotel. When he arrived I failed to recognise him until he introduced himself. He was about forty-five, but the war had turned him into an old man; pale, thin, unkempt and with a hunted look about him. Pfender was a staunch anti-Nazi, who was nearly sent to a concentration camp because he refused to have Hitler's portrait in his office.

I hustled him up to my room without telling the officer who was in charge of the hotel. Pfender was literally starving, but the only food I had in my room was a tin of Army issue dripping.

'Do you mind if I eat it now?' he asked, and he finished the whole tin there and then.

Pfender, a strict Roman Catholic and family man, had been a chief engineer with the Boerzig Company. I had seen him once during the war, after I sent a letter to him, posted by an agent in Sweden, arranging to meet him in neutral territory in Lisbon.

My intention was to enlist him in acts of sabotage within his own German factories, which made armaments and locomotives. Although he was anti-Nazi, he was afraid to take action and I could not blame him.

Through General Mining, I had links with Boerzig before the war. They were not a pleasant firm to deal with. I recall the last time Sir George Albu and I went to their headquarters, to buy equipment, and we were met at the railway station by an official limousine, flying a Nazi pennon and with two uniformed SS outriders. Alongside the factory was a park in which we could see benches marked as not for Jews. Boerzig's chairman, Von Wessig, gave us an effusive welcome and he was taken aback when Sir George referred to the park benches and said he would no longer do business with a country which discriminated against Jews in that way. The German immediately picked up a telephone and spoke to one of the government departments.

'We are losing a major contract because of the park benches,' he said, and while we were in his office the offending signs were removed. An hour later the signs were back. It was a stupid and futile gesture because it made no difference to Sir George. We went elsewhere for the supplies.

Most of Boerzig's senior employees were committed Nazis, and Pfender's neck was saved only by the fact that he was such a good engineer. Practically all the other Germans I interviewed in Berlin in 1945 had been Hitler supporters, although none of them confessed the fact. Pat O'Reilly, our Intelligence Officer, was in Hamburg and he telephoned me to say a Dr Bahr had given my name as a reference and said I could vouch for him as I had met him before the war.

'Yes, I know him,' I said. 'He worked for Boerzig and is the worst kind of Nazi.'

The effrontery of the man! He evidently thought, because we had done business in peacetime, I owed him a favour. Yet he had boasted to me about the gold medallion he possessed, signifying his founder membership of the Nazi party.

*

Later in 1945 General Templer was appointed Director of Military Government in occupied Germany. I had returned to London and received a telephone call at my flat, from Templer's adjutant. He said the general wanted me to join his administrative staff and I would be promoted. The prospect did not appeal to me.

'No, thank you,' I replied. 'I've had enough of the Army and SOE. I want to get out as quickly as possible.'

However, there would be little I could do if Templer served a Movement Order on me, commanding me to go to Germany. I hurried round to see our medical officer, who was a good sport. 'Find something wrong with me,' I urged him. 'They are trying to send me back.'

He examined me thoroughly and said, 'Sorry, chum, there's nothing wrong with you.' Then he thought for a moment and added, 'By the way, how do you feel if you eat something very greasy?'

'Awful. Absolutely awful.'

'There *could* be something wrong with your stomach. I'll send you to St Thomas's Hospital for investigation.'

And that was how I missed the Movement Order which would have sent me to Germany. By the time I was discharged from hospital Templer had made other arrangements. Of course, St Thomas's, after exhaustive tests, gave me a clean bill of health.

The next time I was in Berlin I went to see General Templer to pay my respects. He was concerned about the way the Russians were body-snatching scientists, especially those who had been working on the development of the atomic bomb, and electronic experts. He asked me for my opinion, unofficially, saying the Germans needed all the brains they could muster in order to build up the nation again because they had to live, even though they had lost the war.

'There are two things I would do, General,' I replied. 'First, I would have a ten to twelve miles wide No-Man's Land, with machine-gun nests, and anyone attempting to cross it would be shot on sight, otherwise the Russians will pinch all the best brains the Germans have got.'

He shook his head and smiled at the thought. 'You can't possibly do that. And what else would you do?'

'Second, to help us, I would create a situation in which German productivity was the same as the English – in other words, make them lazy.'

'And how would you do that?'

'I would reduce the price of beer; I would make attendance at football matches compulsory; I would cut their working week to four days – and in about ten years they would be on a level with the British.'

Templer blew a cloud of cigarette smoke. 'Balls!' he exclaimed. 'That is something you could never do.'

My suggestions may have sounded facetious, but in a way I was right. If we could have reduced the German diligence, productivity and pathological involvement in whatever they were doing, we would have found them far less competitive in the postwar years.

Another encounter with Templer occurred at the War Office soon after he was appointed Director of Military Intelligence. He sent for me and said, 'I want to ask you a question. Do you think the Russians will get an atomic bomb and, if so, how long do you think it will take them to make one?'

The question surprised me. 'General,' I answered, 'you either consider me a Russian spy, in which case I must be a very inefficient one in your eyes if you believe I would tell you what I know; or else your own intelligence system is no damn good.'

'Mandy, I want to know what you think personally.'

'Very well, General. How long did it take the Americans to develop an atomic bomb?'

'Something like six years.'

'Well, the Russians, with the knowledge they've already acquired through espionage and with their complete disregard for the sanctity of human life, will most probably take two or three years.'

Templer frowned. 'Oh, I don't know about that.'

But I was correct in my assumption that the Russians' highly competent spy network and their body-snatching of German scientists would enable them to halve the time taken by the Americans.

Soviet Russia has always had an offensive-defensive outlook on world affairs, an attitude which became even more entrenched as a result of the devastation and the enormous number of casualties suffered in the Second World War. This is the thinking behind their 'buffer zone' annexation of once-sovereign countries which border the Motherland and which are now firmly under the heel of the USSR, including my own birthplace in the Baltic States. The same attitude has coloured Russian thinking way back to the days of Peter the Great and beyond. For this reason I am convinced the Soviet Union will not launch a Third World War. A contributory factor is the risk war would pose to so many people who have worked their way up to senior positions within the Communist Party. They have prestige, they have power and they have the lucrative perquisites that go with their jobs, which they can cling to until they die, or are deposed.

But these arguments do not preclude the Soviet's avowed aim of world domination, which they seek to achieve through covert means. This has been illustrated dramatically in many countries by support of Marxist leaders and by the backing given to terrorist groups, either directly or through third parties.

It can also be seen also in the disruption caused in vital industries of Western nations by comparatively small numbers of 'activists', aided and abetted by 'sympathetic' politicians. Such people are adept at coercing lethargic union members into disputes which grow out of all proportion to the original grievances. The reason for such disputes is immaterial. After all, the first principle of a Communist take-over is still to create chaos, out of which they believe they can snatch power.

In Britain, if control cannot be achieved through the unions or by political means, I believe a possible approach towards the setting up of a Communist state might be through Ireland. This would be done by the involvement of terrorists, and not necessarily the IRA. Already we have seen the way IRA members and other terrorists have been trained in Libya, and the way in which Cuban assistance has been given to a variety of terrorist causes, helped by Russian funds and expertise. Ireland could become the UK's Cuba, used as a stepping stone in the take-over of mainland Britain.

There can be no doubt about the Soviets' ultimate intentions. The response of the British Foreign Office to these and other world events has always been to adopt a variation of the three monkeys approach: hear all, see all, say nothing. Members of its staff have carved upon their hearts the words, 'Never apologise. Never explain.' Thus, the most terrible of mistakes, the most incompetent of decisions, the most traitorous of people are covered in a cloak of silence. In fairness, its officials have been responsible for much good work throughout the world, but, without the facts, outsiders are unable to assess the true value of the work carried out in that Whitehall ivory tower.

The tortuous ways of the FO are completely alien to me. My background and experience in business have instilled in me a hatred of pomposity and cant. I have never suffered fools gladly, and yet I hope I have been able to recognise merit, and to reward good work as quickly as I have castigated bad.

No doubt I shall be accused of having a chip upon my shoulder, but there have been many occasions, during the war and afterwards, when I have felt the cold hand of Whitehall. For example, after the capture of the *Gazcon* General Gubbins and Sir Charles Hambro both suggested I should be awarded the DSO, but this was whittled down, first to OBE and then to MBE (Military Division). The haggling made me reluctant to accept any recognition and my medal was sent to me in the post. I have never mentioned the MBE award on my visiting cards or in my business dealings. Thirty years after the *Gazcon* affair, in a letter from the Prime Minister's office, I was told my name was to be included in the New Year Honours' List as an OBE.

I declined the honour, replying that, although the offer gave me pleasure, I felt I could not accept it as I did not intend to continue living in Britain. Once you refuse you are never asked again. Some time later I was reliably informed that my firm was to be given the Queen's award for our services in many parts of the world, an award which I am sure was 'blacked' by Foreign Office intervention. L.H.

Manderstam & Co. did, however, receive a Gold Award for Industry from the Organisation of African Unity, for services in Ethiopia.

I was but one of the many who felt slighted by Whitehall's refusal adequately to acknowledge the value of our work. There was, during and after the war, a marked reluctance to recognise with awards the achievements of SOE members. Even our chief, Gubbins, was described by Templer as the least decorated, by his own country, of our senior soldiers and yet he was among the most honoured by foreign governments. He held fourteen foreign decorations, from all the principal Allied powers except the USSR. His MC was won in the First World War, his DSO came from the Norwegian campaign, and for his SOE exploits and leadership he was made, somewhat belatedly, KCMG.

At our passing out parade, when the war was over, Gubbins said to us, 'Our casualties in a physical sense have been high, but we are all emotional casualties. It will take us a long time to recover our emotional equilibrium after this.'

That was true. I believe the post-war rate of divorces amongst those who served in SOE was the highest of all the branches of the Armed Forces. Our people had lived on lies and found it hard to readjust to a peacetime family existence. We came from ordinary civilian backgrounds, or purely military ones, and yet we were programmed for deceit. To live a lie, day in day out, is a very difficult thing. Gradually you condition yourself to a completely different way of thinking and you develop reflexes which in normal circumstances would be regarded as criminal. For months after the war I had to restrain an urge to open desk drawers and check the contents whenever I was left alone in someone else's office.

The pressure on my own marriage was unbearable. I could not give my wife any hint about where I was going or what I was doing. When I was overseas, my letters to her were sent through the Diplomatic Bag system and were posted in Britain. But, as I could not tell the truth, a certain amount of dishonesty crept into the letters. People who had been captured, and particularly those who had been in the hands of the Gestapo, were in a far worse state. They were emotionally, and sometimes physically, shattered. It was no wonder the divorce rate was so high.

Major L. H. Manderstam.

Yalta. The Big Three Conference, when the Russian prisoners' fate was sealed. Winston Churchill, President Roosevelt and Marshal Stalin, seated. Behind are Lord Leather, Anthony Eden, Mr Stettinius, Sir Alexander Cadogan, Mr Molotov and Mr Averill Harriman (US Ambassador to USSR). 9 February 1945.

(*Left*) George Hill, SOE's man in Moscow. (*Right*) Manderstam arriving in Cairo for a business conference.

I had left my first wife in South Africa and I met my second, Ruth, in London shortly before the war. We married when I was home on leave. While it lasted, my wartime second marriage might well be described as a happy co-existence. I am reminded of the description of Nicholas II as an ideal husband, inasmuch as he used always to reply, 'Yes, darling,' to everything his wife said, and then he did exactly the opposite.

CHAPTER NINETEEN

Back in Business

I breathed a sigh of relief when I mothballed my uniform and placed it in the deeper recesses of a wardrobe. At last I could get back to my own business. I had registered a company in 1941, during a spell of leave which was granted to me, officially, to enable me to complete a technical project for General Mining. In fact I had made up my mind to leave General Mining in order to build up my own practice as a consultant, using the £15,000 compensation paid to me by Sir George Albu. It was a humble beginning, with a staff of one, Lionel Warner, who looked after the company's affairs when SOE required my services elsewhere.

Our first contract was with Western Margarine, who had a factory in Acton, London. The way I arrived for the interview, wearing a staff officer's uniform and lolling in a War Office car with a FANY driver at the wheel, caused a stir and may have helped to clinch the deal. The Army driver, of course, had no idea what I was up to and probably thought it had something to do with security. I was called in by Western Margarine because the firm had problems with a hydrogenation plant, which took liquid oil and saturated it and then, under pressure, converted it into margarine. The difficulties centred on a superheater, which we discovered had a design fault. We redesigned it. At the end of the war I took on another man, Peter Wilson, plus two secretaries, and soon I was working a regular twelve hours a day, seven days a week.

When I started my consultancy practice we were concerned only with vegetable oil, because that was the business I knew best. As time went on I realised it was essential to diversify if we were to expand. We moved into gas, steel, North Sea oil and we took on experts in each of these and other fields. We became involved in projects in more than forty countries, concentrating on the Middle East, Far East and Africa.

My company headquarters have always been in London, although the bulk of our business has been conducted in other countries. A main reason for this has been the nature of our activities as consultants, but it is partly due to the suffocating influence of the Old Boy network. The Oxbridge factor may not be as strong as it was, yet Whitehall and the captains of industry have still not become completely reconciled to the age of comprehensive schools and redbrick universities, let alone foreign-born entrepreneurs.

When I was trying to establish my business the world of commerce was still very much Empire-orientated. London was the hub and the titled directors of companies met in St James's clubs to pass on information and to arrange business deals. It was comforting for them to able to label a person instantly. I was the awkward one, and it rankled. The attitudes which encouraged me to go outside the British Isles for business, and to seek it without the aid of the Old Boy network and the official London-based agencies, was of great benefit to my group of companies because trade within the UK shrank, forcing almost all industrial concerns to develop overseas markets. Those of us who had already built up our foreign business, and proved our worth with successful contracts, had a big advantage, especially as we had also established friendly relations with industrial and political leaders in many countries.

My business was founded, and is still conducted, on a very simple basis. Salesmanship is the top priority, and one can always find people to do the job if one pays more. A display of wealth inspires confidence and another essential is to establish a personal relationship with clients, but always to use tact when dealing with them.

A sense of humour also comes in handy. But it is imperative to do one's homework before using it on a client.

I went to negotiate a big contract with Ceylon, where the Industry Minister handling the arrangements was G.G. Ponnambalam. I found out Ponnambalam was a Cambridge graduate and a barrister, who hated South Africans. He already knew something of my background and opened our interview in an aggressive and unpleasant manner.

'I don't like you! I don't like South Africans and I don't like consultants,' he began. 'What is your name again?'

'Manderstam.'

'I shall never be able to pronounce it. I shall call you Amsterdam.'

He was trying to gall and belittle me. From the stories I had heard I knew he liked a joke and so I took a chance.

'Excellency, what is your name?'

The question caught him off guard and he looked at me askance. He was well aware I knew his name, but he replied, 'Ponnambalam.'

'Sorry, sir. I shall never be able to pronounce it. May I call you perambulator?'

He paused for a moment and then burst out laughing. We ended the interview on first-name terms, promising to do all we could to help one another.

We were consultants on the building of two factories in Ceylon/ Sri Lanka. The first was a chemicals complex to produce caustic soda, chlorine and DDT and when I discussed it with Ponnambalam, who was the leader of the Tamil Congress, he made clear I would not get the contract unless I recommended that the factory should be built in the Tamil-dominated northern area of Jaffna. My report was couched in diplomatic terms. The principal market for caustic soda and chlorine was in Colombo, I wrote, which had four times the population of Jaffna and which at first glance appeared to be the natural site for the factory. But if there were other considerations of national interest, including a need to reduce unemployment in certain areas, the government must make its own choice of location. To no one's surprise, Ponnambalam chose Jaffna.

*

Perhaps the biggest adventure of my postwar business life began one afternoon in 1957, when I was browsing through some papers in my London hedquarters. The switchboard girl informed me Washington was on the line and would I speak to them? Intrigued, I took the call, which was from Dr Paul Rykens, a director of Unilever and an old friend of mine.

'Mandy,' he said without preamble, 'I'm sitting in the office of Mr Black, the chairman of the World Bank, and you are coming to work for us.'

'Not on your life!' was my immediate reaction. And then, of

course, I wanted to know what it was all about, especially as Paul seemed in a high state of excitement. He cut short my questions.

'No time to explain,' he said. 'I'm sure you'll do it when you hear what we have in mind. Much better if I see you personally. I shall be at your office tomorrow morning.'

Good as his word, he arrived the next day to offer me control, as Director of Operations, of a new consortium which was being set up by industrialists and bankers with the objective of selling and financing projects in the Middle East. The scheme was supported by the World Bank – officially the International Bank for Reconstruction and Development – and it was a challenge I could not refuse. They provided me with £5,000 a year, tax free, plus an unlimited expense account, a suite at The George Hotel, Beirut, and a car with a chauffeur, all of which added up to a very attractive proposition.

The headquarters of MIDEC (Middle Eastern Development and Economic Corporation) were established in Beirut and I arranged to leave someone else in charge of my own business affairs for two years. Paul Rykens had been the chairman of Unilever NV and MIDEC was his brainchild. It was a prestige operation and, no doubt encouraged by Paul Rykens's participation and by the World Bank's blessing, some of the biggest international companies had fingers in the pie, including such giants as Shell. But despite all this high-powered support, the venture misfired and in two years we managed to pull off only two major projects. This was not due to failure on my part, or by any other individual. The whole concept was wrong, because there was too much conflict of interests. It was impossible to reconcile the demands of the bankers, the contractors, the equipment suppliers and the industrialists. To illustrate the diversity, in banking alone our members included the Dresden Bank, the Deutsche Bank, the Middle Eastern Bank, Barclays Bank, the Standard Bank and the National Bank of South Africa. When we had a development project lined up we circularised all our members, and immediately we had a rush of organisations trying to take part, for their own profit. There is no sentiment in business.

According to the original idea, when a big project turned up one of our members would, for example, offer to supply the equipment, another would provide the services, and a third would find the necessary finance. In practice, because we had too many members in the various financial and industrial fields, there was cut-throat competition.

I had feared this selfish attitude would be a main drawback of the scheme and had said so when I addressed an assembly of Egyptian industrialists and other businessmen on the subject of investment. There were several unquantifiable ingredients which were essential in an industrial society, I explained, including the enforceability of contracts, an honest Civil Service and the acceptance of the dignity of labour. This last concept was perhaps the most difficult for Egyptian businessmen to understand. Arabs have their own very strong code of honour and dignity. In Cairo they looked at me as if I were mad when I said that, during my time as a works manager, I would have thought myself a failure if I could not do any job on the factory floor; if I could not take the foreman's place at an instant's notice and do his work better than he could himself.

Among the irreconcilable problems facing Paul Rykens's scheme was the lack of a common judicial system in the countries in which our developments were proposed. We could not build up an industrial society covering such a large expanse when contracts could not be enforced throughout the area.

As Director of Operations, I was supposed to mediate between the warring factions, but the task would have defeated Solomon. The dream became a nightmare.

When I resumed full control of my company I found its affairs in a shambles, with a heavy overdraft. I had to sell my house in Westbourne Terrace, London, cash-in my insurance policies and start again, virtually from scratch. We pulled out of the crisis and found contracts to make our business solvent once more. In fact we became the leaders in the field. And the man who gave us that accolade was the doyen of the profession, Sir Frederick Warner, the eminent chemical engineering consultant and Fellow of the Royal Society. A feature article in *Chemical Age* magazine quoted him as saying he thought Manderstam and Partners were probably the most successful consulting firm in the business. The article added, 'Manderstam, he says, has shown acute political sense and forged strong links with developing countries like Indonesia and Greece.'

My connections with Indonesia, however, did not get off to a very good start, partly due to the emphasis I placed on salesmanship. We had a brilliant salesman, whose big fault was that he sold services we could not supply. I was on crutches after a hip operation when he telephoned me from Jakarta, saying President Suharto was prepared to sign a contract, but I must arrive in Indonesia not later than 4 June, which gave me forty-eight hours to travel eight thousand miles in the days before regular Jumbo jet flights. I made it, still on crutches, and to my chagrin we did not get the job, which was to act as consultants on the rehabilitation of Indonesian industry.

Some good came out of the trip, however. I got to know leading Indonesians, including the president, and the friendships I made led to a number of business deals between the Indonesians and my company, mostly involving gas and oil. The most important contract was for the redesign and rebuilding of an old Russian steel mill in West Java.

In contacts with oriental, African and Asian people one must always remember not to use the same yardsticks as are applied to the average Westerner, and the difference in attitudes to women is most marked. When President Suharto received me in his palace we talked about ways in which Indonesia's economy could be improved. If the purchasing power of his 130 million subjects were increased by only two dollars a head, an extra 260 million dollars' worth of trade would be generated, I pointed out.

'And how would you do that?'

'Change the status of women. If each of your married men had a nagging wife, pestering him for another pair of shoes, a new dress, or more food, you would soon increase productivity and spending power.'

When President Suharto came to Britain for a State Visit in 1979 I was among those who received a Special Invitation to go to Buckingham Palace to meet him. My legs, as usual, were not in good shape and there were ninety steps to climb to the reception area. After dinner I had an urgent need to empty my bladder and I asked one of the palace staff to direct me to the nearest toilet. It was downstairs, and I could not see how I could manage to get down all those steps and back again.

The royal servant noticed my discomfiture and came across to me. 'There's another place,' he whispered. 'If you press that button over there, a concealed door will open. It's a facility used by Prince Philip.' It gave me much satisfaction to know I was gaining relief through sharing Prince Philip's facility.

I have never rated very highly the back-up given by the British government to assist businessmen in their dealings overseas. But the British Embassy was among the first places at which I called on my missions to foreign countries. Even when the Embassy staff could not help, they could do a lot of harm if you did not get them on your side.

Old acquaintances were renewed and fresh ones made through contacts with the various Embassies. Yet there were times when echoes from the past could be disconcerting for one or other of the parties involved. On a business trip to Cairo I went to a British Embassy reception, to which the Russian envoys were invited. I shall never forget the look of disbelief on the face of one of the senior Russians when we met, for he was none other than Kiselnikov, who was a member of my schoolboy gang in Nizhni Novgorod. We used to pick fights and get into all kinds of scrapes. I still have a photograph showing the pair of us in our post-Revolution days.

'Hello,' I said. 'Fancy seeing you after all this time.'

He blenched. 'Please be careful what you say and do not mention the old times,' he said. 'You know I am at the Embassy.'

In looking back over my business career it pleases me to know that much of my work has contributed to Third World economies. I am, however, apprehensive about the future of Third World nations, and especially those in Africa, where corruption touches everyone from the presidential staff to the most junior Customs official, and where contracts have to include a percentage to cover bribes. I have similar fears for those areas which have become totally dependent on oil revenues, acquired too easily. There are tremendous dangers in basing a nation's wealth on one product, no matter how boundless and valuable the product apears to be. My own view is that the Arabs may drown themselves in oil, an assumption which derives from my knowledge of work being done on oil substitutes, the economies likely to be achieved in oil usage, the exploitation of supplies from non-Arab areas and the growth in the use of nuclear and other forms of energy. The United Kingdom, one should remember, has its own oil, natural gas and nuclear power and, perhaps most important, has an enormous stock of coal for use as fuel and to be exploited as a raw material in the manufacture of a thousand and one essential products.

I have always loved the English, with their charming hypocrisy, and nothing gave me greater pleasure than to be accepted as an honorary Englishman when I settled among the orchards and hop-gardens of Kent, the most English of counties. After all, I had served the country in wartime and made it my home for forty years. My acceptance was complete when a single incident confirmed my status as the village eccentric. It happened on a night when my wife, Muriel, had gone to the Glyndebourne opera and I was sitting on a bed, surrounded by six dachshunds at our home in Sevenoaks Weald, cleaning a Colt pistol I had retained after the war. I committed an offence that deserved a court martial, leaving a round 'up the spout.' It went off and the bullet ripped through one of my fingers. Blood spurted everywhere, while the dogs hurtled off the bed quicker than I had ever seen them move. A woman doctor who answered my telephone call for help obviously thought I was insane as the shock, relief and humour of the situation made me cackle with hysterial laughter.

I had taken part in the Russian Revolution on both sides; I had served in the Red Army and survived the Lubianka; I had been a secret agent in Africa and Europe and worked in some of the most unsavoury places on earth, yet not until I was seventy did I shoot and injure anyone – and the victim was myself.

APPENDIX

SOE recommended, on 26 September 1944, the award of the OBE to Major Manderstam for his Gazcon operation, but he was made an MBE.

The recommendation stated:

Major L.H. MANDERSTAM was responsible for the preliminary work and for planning the operation which resulted in the capture at sea by the Royal Navy of the Vichy ship *Gazcon* on 8 September 1941, which had been lying in the Port of Lobito, Angola, Portuguese West Africa.

He worked single-handed to effect all the arrangements:

(a) To suborn the captain of the ship, which required considerable tact and diplomacy.

(b) To prevent the scuttling of the ship by the rabid pro-Nazi second-in-command, by visiting it with the Harbour-Master to gather information, inspect the position of sea-cocks, etc., which entailed considerable risk in a neutral port under the eyes of an armed guard and the International Police, and by inducing seven members of the crew to sign on as Free Frenchmen and arming some of them.

(c) To pay £10,000 to the captain to proceed to the rendezvous with the R.N.; this payment he arranged by borrowing the money on his own responsibility and by sheer effontery did so from a business man who was highly suspect and whose wife was reported to be a German agent. He insisted on the money being paid in small denominations, so that eventually the captain agreed to receive a cheque payable in America, and Major Manderstam returned the money to the lender.

(d) Throughout the whole of the planning, Major Manderstam exercised great skill, judgement, tact and balance of mind, with the result that the operation was completely successful. The *Gazcon* was valued at £106,000 and her cargo approximately £300,000.

Bibliography

Victims of Yalta, Nikolai Tolstoy (Hodder & Stoughton 1977).

The Last Secret, Nicholas Bethell (Andre Deutsch, 1974).

Moscow Mission, Lt.Gen. Walter Bedell Smith (Wm Collins, 1950).

The Gulag Archipelago, Alexander Solzhenitsyn (Wm Collins, 1973).

The White Rabbit, Bruce Marshall (Evans Bros., 1952).

Chronicles of Wasted Time, Vol. 2, The Infernal Grove, Malcolm Muggeridge (Collins, 1973).

My Silent War, H.A.R. (Kim) Philby (Grove Press, New York, 1968).

Disaster at Bari, Glenn B. Infield (Robert Hale, 1974).

Thanks are due to Messrs Heinemann for permission to quote from *Moscow Mission*, to Lord Bethell and Messrs Andre Deutsch from *The Last Secret*, to Count Nikolai Tolstoy and Messrs Hodder & Stoughton from *Victims of Yalta* and to Messrs Collins from *The Gulag Archipelago*.

Index